TABLE OF CONTENTS

Page

# ACRONYMS

| | |
|---|---|
| AOC | Alliance of Civilizations |
| AQ | al-Qaida |
| AQI | al-Qaida in Iraq |
| CSIS | Center for Strategic and International Studies |
| DNI | Director of National Intelligence |
| EIJ | Egyptian Islamic Jihad |
| FATA | Federally Administered Tribal Areas (Pakistan) |
| GWOT | Global War on Terrorism |
| ICU | Islamic Courts Union (Somalia) |
| JI | Jemaah Islamiyah (Indonesia) |
| NGO | Nongovernmental Organization |
| NIC | National Intelligence Council |
| NIE | National Intelligence Estimate |
| NMSP-WOT | *National Military Strategic Plan for the War on Terrorism 2006* |
| NSCT | *National Strategy for Combating Terrorism September 2006* |
| NSS | *The National Security Strategy of the United States of America March 2006* |
| OEF | Operation Enduring Freedom (Afghanistan) |
| OIF | Operation Iraqi Freedom |
| QDR | Quadrennial Defense Report |
| UBL | Usama bin Laden |
| UN | United Nations |
| US | United States |

# CHRONOLOGY

| | |
|---|---|
| 570-632 | Birth of Muhammed; Islamic expansion to Arabian Peninsula (622-632) |
| 632-661 | Expansion of Caliphate to Syria, Palestine and North Africa |
| 661-750 | Expansion of Caliphate to Spain, Portugal and Southern Italy |
| 1099 | Capture of Jerusalem by the Crusaders |
| 1187 | Saladin captures Jerusalem from the Crusaders |
| 1224 | Tartars begin conquest of Russia |
| 1258 | Mongols conquer Baghdad; destroy Abbasid Caliphate |
| 1263-1328 | Taqi ad-Din ibn Tamiyya born present-day Turkey; moves to Damascus |
| 1300 | Expansion begins under Ottoman Empire |
| 1453 | Ottoman Empire captures Constantinople; end of Byzantine Empire |
| 1480 | Muscovite Russia ends Tartar dominance in Russia |
| 1492 | Spanish Reconquista completed with conquest of Grenada |
| 1683 | Europeans defeat Ottoman armies in Vienna; end of Ottoman expansion |
| 1703-1792 | Muhamad ibn 'Abd al-Wahhab born Saudi Arabia; founder of Wahhabism |
| 1798 | Napoleon conquers Egypt; beginning of modern Middle Eastern history |
| 1800s | European imperialism begins in Middle East |
| 1906-1949 | Hassan al-Banna born in Egypt; founder Muslim Brotherhood; killed 1949 |
| 1906-1966 | Sayyid Qutb born in Egypt; leading extremist ideologue; executed 1966 |
| 1918 | WWI ends; defeat of Ottoman Empire; territory divided among Europeans |
| 1923 | Modern state of Turkey founded; Mustafa Kemal (Ataturk) first President |
| 1924 | Ataturk abolishes caliphate |
| 1925 | Sheikh Abd al-Aziz Ibn Saud captures Mecca and Medina, Saudi Arabia |

| | |
|---|---|
| 1932 | Abd al-Aziz Ibn Saud establishes Kingdom of Saudi Arabia |
| 1930s | Oil discovered in Saudi Arabia |
| 1948 (May) | State of Israel established; Israel subsequently defeats Arab armies |
| 1948 (Dec) | Egyptian Prime Minister Mahmud Fahmi al-Nuqrashi assassinated |
| 1949 | Hassan al-Banna killed, allegedly by police, after Muslim Brotherhood member assassinated Egyptian Prime Minister |
| 1951-- | Ayman al-Zawahiri born in Egypt; leader of Egyptian Islamic Jihad |
| 1953 | Shah takes power in Iran after coup |
| 1957-- | Usama bin Laden born in Saudi Arabia; founder of al-Qaida |
| 1964 | Sayyid Qutb publishes manifesto *Milestones* |
| 1966 | Sayyid Qutb hanged for plotting against the Egyptian government |
| 1967 | Israel defeats combined Arab armies in Six-Day War |
| 1972 | Munich Olympic massacre |
| 1973 | Arab-Israeli War; oil crisis empowers oil-producing Arab states |
| 1979 (Feb) | Iranian Revolution |
| 1979 (Apr) | Egyptians vote to approve peace treaty with Israel |
| 1979 (Nov) | Iran hostage crisis |
| 1979 (Nov) | Grand Mosque seizure in Mecca, Saudi Arabia |
| 1979 (Dec) | Soviet invasion of Afghanistan |
| 1980-88 | Iran-Iraq War |
| 1981 (Oct) | Assassination of Egyptian President Anwar Sadat |
| 1983 (Apr) | Bombing of US Embassy in Beirut |
| 1983 (Oct) | Bombing of US Marine barracks in Beirut |

| | |
|---|---|
| 1985 (Oct) | Achille Lauro hijacking in eastern Mediterranean |
| 1989 (Feb) | Last Soviet forces withdraw from Afghanistan |
| 1991 (Feb) | Defeat of Saddam Hussein in Gulf War |
| 1991 (Dec) | Collapse of Soviet Union |
| 1991 (Dec) | Algerian elections postponed fearing extremist victory; violence ensues |
| 1993 (Feb) | First World Trade Center bombing |
| 1993 (Oct) | Battle of Mogadishu, Somalia |
| 1996 (Jun) | Khobar Towers bombing in Saudi Arabia |
| 1996 (Aug) | Usama bin Laden issues fatwa *Declaration of War against the Americans Occupying the Land of the Two Holy Places* |
| 1997 (Nov) | Luxor massacre in Egypt |
| 1998 (Feb) | Usama bin Laden, Ayman al-Zawahiri, et al. issue *World Islamic Front Declaration of Jihad against the Jews and the Crusaders* |
| 1998 (Aug) | US Embassy Bombings in Tanzania and Kenya |
| 2000 (Oct) | USS Cole bombed in Yemeni port |
| 2001 (Jun) | Al-Qaida and Egyptian Islamic Jihad complete merger |
| 2001 (Sep) | 11 September 2001 terrorist attacks against the US |
| 2001 (Oct) | Start of war in Afghanistan (Operation Enduring Freedom) |
| 2001 (Dec) | Zawahiri publishes AQ manifesto *Knights Under the Prophet's Banner* |
| 2002 (Oct) | Bali bombings in Indonesia |
| 2002 (Oct) | Chechen rebels seize a Moscow theater |
| 2002 (Oct) | Usama bin Laden releases letter *To the Americans* |
| 2003 (Mar) | Start of war in Iraq (Operation Iraqi Freedom) |
| 2003 (Dec) | Two assassination attempts against Pakistani President Musharraf |

| | |
|---|---|
| 2004 (Mar) | Madrid train bombings |
| 2004 (Sep) | Beslan school hostage crisis in North Ossetia, Russia |
| 2005 (Jul) | London public transportation system bombings |
| 2006 (Feb) | Al-Askari (Golden) mosque bombing in Samarra, Iraq |
| 2006 (Jun) | Al-Qaida in Iraq leader Abu Musab al-Zarqawi killed in Iraq |
| 2006 (Jun) | Islamic Courts Union (ICU) seizes Somali capital |
| 2006 (Aug) | British foil alleged plot to detonate explosives on planes mid-flight to US |
| 2006 (Sep) | Pakistan reaches accords with Islamic militants in Waziristan |
| 2006 (Dec) | ICU ousted by combined Somali and Ethiopian offensive |

# CHAPTER 1

## INTRODUCTION

> This is the challenge of our time. This is the call of a generation, to stand against the extremists and support moderate leaders across the broader Middle East, to help us all secure a future of peace. (2006, 45)
>
> President George W. Bush, Speech to Reserve Officers Association

### Background

The United States is a nation at war. It will be a long war. The terrorist attacks on 11 September 2001 carried out by nineteen Arab Muslim men were the catalyst that brought the US to this war: the Global War on Terrorism (GWOT). Since then, Americans have asked themselves why these men would carry out such attacks.

The terrorist attacks on 11 September 2001 were the most spectacular and deadly of a long and growing list of terrorist attacks against the US and the West by Islamic extremists. However, US and coalition responses to Islamic extremism since 11 September 2001 have not prevailed and in some cases have exacerbated the problem of Islamic radicalization even further. Therefore, in a broader sense, the question is, What is it that causes Islamic extremists to carry out terrorist attacks against the US and the West? or What are the root causes or sources of Islamic extremism?

There are many sources of Islamic extremism; not all are widely accepted or understood. In October 2005, President Bush said, "Over the years these extremists have used a litany of excuses for violence; the Israeli presence on the West Bank, the US military presence in Saudi Arabia, the defeat of the Taliban, or the Crusades of a thousand years ago" (4).

Understanding the sources of Islamic extremism is critically important to designing a viable long-term strategy to counter or eliminate them. Have US policy makers correctly identified the sources of Islamic extremism? *The National Security Strategy of the United States of America March 2006 (NSS)* and other current US government documents, international organizations, nongovernmental organizations (NGOs) and civilian experts, and Islamic extremists identify different sources of Islamic extremism. The following four examples are illustrative of the sources as identified by the different groups. The purpose of presenting these perspectives is not to advocate or criticize any one point of view, but rather to highlight the differences of opinion that exist and to demonstrate the challenges associated with finding common ground among disparate groups in identifying the sources of Islamic extremism.

The *NSS* identifies four sources of Islamic extremism which lead to acts of terrorism: political alienation, grievances that can be blamed on others, subcultures of conspiracy and misinformation, and an ideology that justifies murder. The strategy also deemphasizes four areas that are typically cited as sources of Islamic extremism: poverty, US policy in Iraq, Israeli-Palestinian issues, and US counterterrorism efforts. The following two excerpts from the *NSS* highlight the government's views.

The terrorism we confront today springs from:

- Political alienation. Transnational terrorists are recruited from people who have no voice in their own government and see no legitimate way to promote change in their own country. Without a stake in the existing order, they are vulnerable to manipulation by those who advocate a perverse vision based on violence and destruction.
- Grievances that can be blamed on others. The failures the terrorists feel and see are blamed on others, and on perceived injustices from the recent or sometimes distant past. The terrorists' rhetoric keeps wounds associated with this past fresh and raw, a potent motivation for revenge and terror.

2

- Sub-cultures of conspiracy and misinformation. Terrorists recruit more effectively from populations whose information about the world is contaminated by falsehoods and corrupted by conspiracy theories. The distortions keep alive grievances and filter out facts that would challenge popular prejudices and self-serving propaganda.
- An ideology that justifies murder. Terrorism ultimately depends upon the appeal of an ideology that excuses or even glorifies the deliberate killing of innocents. A proud religion – the religion of Islam – has been twisted and made to serve an evil end, as in other times and places other religions have been similarly abused.

To wage this battle of ideas effectively, we must be clear-eyed about what does and does not give rise to terrorism:

- Terrorism is not the inevitable by-product of poverty. Many of the September 11 hijackers were from middle-class backgrounds, and many terrorist leaders, like bin Laden, are from privileged upbringings.
- Terrorism is not simply a result of hostility to US policy in Iraq. The United States was attacked on September 11th and earlier, well before we toppled the Saddam Hussein regime. Moreover, countries that stayed out of the Iraq war have not been spared from terror attack.
- Terrorism is not simply a result of Israeli-Palestinian issues. Al-Qaida plotting from the September 11th attacks began in the 1990s, during an active period in the peace process.
- Terrorism is not simply a response to our efforts to prevent terror attacks. The al-Qaida network targeted the United States long before the United States targeted al-Qaida. Indeed, the terrorists are emboldened more by perceptions of weakness than by demonstrations of resolve. Terrorists lure recruits by telling them that we are decadent and easily intimidated and will retreat if attacked. (White House 2006, 9-10)

In its November 2006 report, the United Nations (UN)-sponsored Alliance of Civilizations (AOC) group (an international panel of 20 world renowned experts) provided a different perspective on the sources of Islamic extremism and concluded that the root of the matter is political not religious.

> In its report, the High-level Group of the Alliance of Civilizations maintains that although religion is often cynically exploited to stir passions, fuel suspicions, and support alarmist claims that the world is facing a new "war of religion", the root of the matter is political.
> Furthermore, the Arab-Israeli conflict has become a critical symbol of the deepening rift. Along with Western military interventions in countries like Iraq

and Afghanistan the Group argues, this conflict contributes significantly to the growing sense of resentment and mistrust that mars relations among communities. The report also suggests that the repression of non-violent political opposition and the slow pace of reforms in some Muslim countries is a key factor in the rise of extremism. (Press Release p. 1)

In 2004, the RAND Corporation, a California-based NGO, prepared a report for

the US Air Force entitled *The Muslim World After 9/11* in which it examined the sources

of Islamic extremism and divided the sources into three classes: conditions, processes,

and catalytic events.

> Conditions include failed political and economic models, structural anti-Westernism, and decentralization of religious authority in Sunni Islam.
> Processes include the Islamic resurgence, Arabization of the non-Arab Muslim world, external funding of religious fundamentalism and extremism, the convergence of Islamism and tribalism, growth of radical Islamic networks, emergence of the mass media, and the Palestinian-Israeli and Kashmir conflicts.
> Catalytic events include the Iranian revolution, the Afghan war, the Gulf War of 1991, September 11 and the Global War on Terrorism, and the Iraq war. (Table O.3, p. 37)

Lastly, Islamic extremists themselves have been forthright about the sources of

their grievances through the use of audio and videotape messages and through Internet

postings. Usama bin Laden and Ayman al-Zawahiri in their 1998 *World Islamic Front*

*Declaration of Jihad against the Jews and the Crusaders* cited three principal grievances:

Saudi Arabia, Iraq, and Israel.

> First, for more than seven years the United States is occupying the lands of Islam in the holiest of its territories, Arabia, plundering its riches, overwhelming its rulers, humiliating its people, threatening its neighbors, and using its bases in the peninsula as a spearhead to fight against the neighboring Islamic peoples.
> Second, despite the immense destruction inflicted on the Iraqi people at the hands of the Crusader-Jewish alliance and in spite of the appalling number of dead, exceeding one million, the Americans, nevertheless, in spite of all this, are trying once more to repeat this dreadful slaughter. It seems that the long blockade following after a fierce war, the dismemberment and destruction are not enough for them. So they come again today to destroy what remains of this people and to humiliate their Muslim neighbors.

Third, while the purposes of the Americans in these wars are religious and economic, they also serve the petty state of the Jews, to divert attention from their occupation of Jerusalem and their killing of Muslims in it. (1-2)

As these four examples show, what different groups identify as the sources of Islamic extremism varies considerably. The purpose of this thesis is to: conduct a qualitative analysis of the sources of Islamic extremism from multiple perspectives (US government, international organizations, NGOs and civilian experts, and Islamic extremists), determine if the *NSS* properly identifies the sources of Islamic extremism, and make recommendations on how to counter the sources of Islamic extremism and improve US security and counterterrorism strategy.

This chapter is organized into seven parts: background; thesis intent and research questions; definition of key terms; scope, limitations and delimitations; significance of study; and summary and conclusions.

## Thesis Intent and Research Questions

The primary research question this thesis seeks to answer is, Has the *NSS* properly identified the sources of Islamic extremism? In order to answer the primary question, secondary questions are needed to provide a complete review of the topic.

Secondary questions include: What do the *NSS* and other US government documents identify as the sources of Islamic extremism? What do international organizations identify as the sources of Islamic extremism? What do NGOs and civilian experts identify as the sources of Islamic extremism? What do Islamic extremists identify as the sources of their grievances?

## Assumptions

There are four assumptions which keep this thesis focused on answering the research questions. First, the GWOT will continue for the foreseeable future; defeating Islamic extremism will require decades of effort. Therefore, a strategic analysis of the sources of Islamic extremism and the development of a corresponding strategy to counter those sources merits further study.

Second, Islamic extremists cannot directly challenge the US militarily and will therefore continue to use terrorism as a tactic. Furthermore, given the free and open nature of US society, extremists will continue to use irregular warfare (to include terrorist attacks) to attack the US homeland and US interests abroad.

Third, while extremists cannot defeat the US militarily, the converse is also true; US military efforts alone cannot prevail against Islamic extremism.

Lastly, whereas Islamic extremists leverage sources of discontent or grievances to recruit new terrorists, this thesis assumes that if properly identified, some sources of Islamic extremism can be countered, mitigated or eliminated.

## Definition of Key Terms

Several key terms used in this thesis are defined below; others are found in the glossary. Of note, the definition of Islamism is drawn generally from the International Crisis Group's 2006 report, *Understanding Islam*.

Apostate. One who has abandoned their religious faith, principles or cause.

Caliphate. Pan-Islamic state.

Globalization. Process of becoming worldwide in scope.

6

Irredentist Islamic extremist. Subset of Islamic extremism; seeks to regain land ruled by non-Muslims or under occupation.

Islamic extremism. Individuals committed to restructuring political society in accordance with their vision of Islamic law and willing to use violence to achieve their goals; three types: irredentist, nationalist and transnational.

Islamism. Islamic activism; three types: political, missionary and extremist.

Jihad. Struggle; two types: individual internal struggle against evil and temptation, and holy war waged by Muslims against infidels.

Jihadist. Muslim involved in a jihad (note: Islamic extremists often identify themselves as jihadists).

Nationalist Islamic Extremist. Subset of Islamic extremism; focus is on combating Muslim governments considered impious or apostate.

Source. Thing or place from which something comes or arises; also origin, root cause.

Terrorism. Premeditated, politically motivated violence perpetrated against noncombatants by subnational groups or clandestine agents.

Transnational Islamic extremist. Subset of Islamic extremism; focus transcends national boundaries; also called global terrorists or global jihadists.

## Scope, Limitations, and Delimitations

The scope of this thesis is limited in several key areas.

First, Muslim diasporas face unique conditions, such as the failure to assimilate, which tend to alter their sources of extremism from those of Muslims in the Middle East and Asia. This thesis does not address the sources of Islamic extremism among Muslim diasporas.

Second, this thesis remains unclassified by using only open source information.

Third, the information cutoff date for research material used in this thesis was 1 January 2007.

Fourth, this thesis standardizes spelling for consistency but does not change spelling used in quotations (e.g., this thesis uses al-Qaida, but the term is also spelled al-Qaeda or Al Qaida). Similarly, the terms Islamic extremists and jihadists are often used interchangeably depending on the point of view. This thesis uses Islamic extremists for consistency, but jihadists is used in certain referenced text.

Significance of Study

Islamic extremists perpetrated the 11 September 2001 attacks, they support the Taliban insurgency in Afghanistan and the insurgency in Iraq, and they constitute 26 of the 42 groups on the State Department's list of foreign terrorist organizations (US Department of State 2006, Ch. 8, p. 1). Islamic extremists are the principal threat in what will be a long war.

Summary and Conclusions

In October 2005, President Bush said, "The murderous ideology of the Islamic radicals is the great challenge of our new century" (4). Further, the *National Military Strategic Plan for the War on Terrorism (2006)* states that violent extremism is the primary threat to the US, its allies, and interests. Given the nature of the threat, it is clear that understanding the sources of Islamic extremism is critically important to designing a strategy to counter or eliminate them. However, the *NSS* and other current US strategy documents, international organizations, NGOs and civilian experts, and Islamic extremists identify different sources of Islamic extremism. This thesis seeks to answer the question, Has the *NSS* properly identified the sources of Islamic extremism? This thesis also aims to determine if there are gaps in US security and counterterrorism strategy, and to make recommendations on how to improve those strategies.

CHAPTER 2

RESEARCH METHODOLOGY

> Liberating the Muslim nation, confronting the enemies of Islam, and launching jihad against them require a Muslim authority, established on a Muslim land that raises the banner of jihad and rallies the Muslims around it. Without achieving this goal our actions will mean nothing more than mere and repeated disturbances that will not lead to the aspired goal, which is the restoration of the caliphate and the dismissal of the invaders from the land of Islam. (Mansfield 2006, 225)
>
> Ayman al-Zawahiri, *Knights Under the Prophet's Banner*

Introduction

The objective of this thesis is to answer the question, Has the *NSS* properly identified the sources of Islamic extremism?

This thesis uses qualitative analysis to answer the primary and secondary research questions. Further, it uses textual analysis (i.e., document studies) to compare and contrast data from multiple perspectives.

To facilitate data reduction, data display, and conclusion drawing, primary and secondary textual source materials are grouped into four categories:

1. *NSS* and other US government documents

2. International Organizations

3. NGOs and Civilian Experts

4. Islamic Extremists

This chapter is organized into six parts: introduction, research questions, frame of reference, grounds for comparison, organizational scheme, and conclusion.

## Research Questions

The primary research question is, Has the *NSS* properly identified the sources of Islamic extremism?

Secondary research questions correspond to the four source material categories. The secondary research questions are: What do the *NSS* and other US government documents identify as the sources of Islamic extremism? What do international organizations identify as the sources of Islamic extremism? What do NGOs and civilian experts identify as the sources of Islamic extremism? What do Islamic extremists identify as the sources of their grievances?

The scope of the research questions is not unlimited. Rather, the research questions are bound by the assumptions, limitations and delimitations covered in Chapter 1, "Introduction."

## Frame of Reference

The *NSS* is the frame of reference against which other source materials are compared and contrasted. Other source materials (e.g., other US government documents, international organizations, nongovernmental sources, and Islamic extremists) used for this research either corroborate, extend, or contradict data found in the *NSS*.

## Grounds for Comparison

In order to answer the primary research question, this thesis takes into consideration the perspectives of four general groups. The rationale behind why these groups are used is that they look at the problem from different angles and, in the case of the US government and Islamic extremists, from opposing sides. Taken together, these perspectives are intended to provide a thorough and complete look at the problem.

The problem of Islamic extremism is a global one. Therefore, the UN as the premier international organization is an important stakeholder and relevant perspective to consider. The decision to include international organizations as a grounds for comparison is bolstered by the fact that the UN General Assembly passed a counterterrorism strategy in September 2006 which addresses the topic of this thesis and that the UN-sponsored AOC group released its final report in November 2006 which included detailed conclusions and recommendations regarding the sources of Islamic extremism and how to combat them.

NGOs and civilian experts provide a unique perspective into the issue of Islamic extremism. Chief among these: they are generally not constrained by the same political considerations as US government and UN policy makers when identifying grievances that may be religious in nature; they have researched the sources of terrorism and extremism thoroughly and have written extensively on the topic; and they inherently have different access to information (e.g., interviews with Islamic extremists) than do governmental sources, which may shed additional light on the subject.

Lastly, the rationale for using Islamic extremists as a group is that they have been forthright in stating their grievances publicly and that understanding the perspective of Islamic extremists is important to understanding the problem from all sides. Usama bin Laden's October 2002 letter *To the Americans* is a good example. Below is a synopsis of the letter's key points from Bruce Lawrence who edited a compilation of bin Laden's statements entitled, *Messages to the World: The Statements of Osama Bin Laden.*

Two features mark the letter out. The first is its succinct but wide-ranging summary of what bin Laden holds to be the political misdeeds of the United States across the Muslim world: in Palestine, Somalia, Chechnya, Kashmir, Lebanon, Iraq, Afghanistan, and not the least in the Arab states that act as its willing agent. The second is a moral and cultural denunciation of American society as a sink of usury, debauchery, drug addiction, gambling, prostitution, and environmental destruction, a result of America's apostasy in separating church and state, and choosing to live by man-made laws rather than those by God. (Lawrence 2005, 160)

Organizational Scheme

This thesis conducts qualitative research by assembling a body of primary and secondary source materials. The source material is divided into four groups: the US government, international organizations, NGOs and civilian experts, and Islamic extremists--which make up the four perspectives from which to compare and contrast data relative to the *NSS*.

The research methodology is organized into three phases: data reduction, data display and conclusion drawing. First, data reduction entails: conducting initial research, narrowing the source materials for the four groups down sufficiently such that the topic is fully covered but not redundant or overwhelming for the reader, and then organizing the research data in a meaningful way.

Second, data display goes beyond data reduction to organize the data in such a way to permit conclusion drawing. This thesis uses the "Literature Review" (Chapter 3) and "Data Display Matrix" (Appendix A) to show what the various organizations and individuals identify the sources of Islamic extremism. The "Literature Review" uses a text-by-text approach to focus and emphasize points taken from the data reduction phase for manageability and to record answers to the secondary research questions. The

"Literature Review" and "Data Display Matrix" also reflect trends, common themes and deviations, which help to answer the research questions.

Lastly, conclusion drawing involves reviewing and analyzing the data to answer the research questions. It involves looking for trends, themes and deviations from the data reduction and data display phases, and then presenting them in Chapter 4, "Analysis," and Chapter 5, "Conclusions and Recommendations," using a thematic approach.

## Conclusion

This thesis seeks to answer the primary research question, Has the *NSS* properly identified the sources of Islamic extremism? It uses qualitative analysis to compare and contrast data from multiple sources to answer the primary and secondary research questions. Using a three-phased process (data reduction, data display, and conclusion drawing), this thesis analyzes the sources of Islamic extremism from multiple perspectives to ensure a thorough and complete review of the problem. Ultimately, it takes the text-by-text analysis of what has been written on the subject in Chapter 3, "Literature Review," and applies that information using a thematic approach in Chapter 4, "Analysis," in order to answer the primary and secondary research questions (Frechtling and Sharp 1997; Walk 1998).

# CHAPTER 3

## LITERATURE REVIEW

> Why are we fighting and opposing you? The answer is very
> simple: because you attacked us and continue to attack us. . . .
> What are we calling you to, and what do we want from you? The
> first thing that we are calling you to is Islam. . . . The second thing
> we call you to, is to stop your oppression, lies, immorality, and
> debauchery that has spread among you. (2002, 1, 3, 4)
>
> Usama bin Laden letter *To the Americans*

### Introduction

The purpose of this thesis is to: conduct a qualitative analysis of the sources of

Islamic extremism from multiple perspectives, determine if the *NSS* properly identifies

the sources of Islamic extremism, and make recommendations on how to counter the

sources of Islamic extremism and improve US security and counterterrorism strategy.

Before and especially after 11 September 2001, much has been said and written

about the sources of Islamic extremism. This chapter reviews the sources of information

used for this thesis research and highlights what each group identifies as the sources of

Islamic extremism in order to answer the secondary research questions. In doing so, the

answers to the secondary research questions should provide the foundation of data

necessary to answer the primary research question. Additionally, this thesis uses data

obtained from the "Literature Review" to facilitate qualitative comparative analysis in

Chapter 4, "Analysis," and conclusion drawing in Chapter 5, "Conclusions and

Recommendations."

This chapter is organized into six parts: introduction; US government; international organizations; NGOs and civilian experts; Islamic extremists; and summary and conclusions.

## US Government

### White House

As mentioned in Chapter 1, "Introduction," the *NSS* identifies four sources of Islamic extremism: political alienation, grievances that can be blamed on others, subcultures of conspiracy and misinformation, and an ideology that justifies murder. The *NSS* also emphasizes the extremists' ideology--the idea of jihad as a call for murder against those individuals that extremists regard as apostates or unbelievers--as being central to the extremists' cause. Further, the strategy describes the extremists' ideology as one that "can turn the disenchanted into murderers willing to kill innocent victims" (2006, 9). The *NSS* contends that the extremist ideology espoused by bin Laden and others is not simply a source of extremism for global-minded extremists, but is also a source of Islamic extremism for disenchanted Muslims caught in a battle of ideas. This premise argues that Muslims are caught in a battle of ideas: on the one hand of tolerance and change associated with globalization and modernization and on the other hand of intolerance and a traditional Islamic system, regressive in the sense that it seeks to emulate the time of the Prophet.

The *NSS* also deemphasizes four areas that are typically cited as sources of Islamic extremism: poverty, US policy in Iraq, Israeli-Palestinian issues, and US efforts to prevent terror attacks. However, while the *NSS* addresses ways to counter each of the four factors it identifies as principal sources of extremism, it does not address ways to counter the four areas that it deemphasized. It may be that some sources of Islamic extremism are immitigable and this thesis will return to this topic in Chapter 5, "Conclusions and Recommendations."

The *National Strategy for Combating Terrorism September 2006 (NSCT)* contains the same verbiage as the *NSS* regarding the sources of Islamic extremism--it identifies the same four principal sources and same four areas of de-emphasis as the *NSS*. Additionally, like the *NSS*, the *NSCT* focuses on the extremists' radical ideology as a source from which terrorism springs.

The *NSCT* makes three other points worth highlighting. First, the strategy notes that extremists seek "to expel Western power and influence from the Muslim world" (2006, 5). Second, it argues that extremists seek to establish regimes that rule according to their "violent and intolerant distortion of Islam" (2006, 5). This, in effect, reflects the extremists' desire to replace regimes they consider apostate or un-Islamic. Lastly, the strategy contends that the aim of some extremists, particularly al-Qaida, is to establish a "single, pan-Islamic, totalitarian regime that stretches from Spain to Southeast Asia" (2006, 5). A historical grievance, this aim reflects a desire by some extremists to reclaim Muslim lands held at the height of Islamic expansion, commonly referred to as the caliphate.

The *NSCT* also notes that there are multiple extremist organizations confronting the US and many of these extremists groups have common grievances and aims (Note: The US State Department lists 42 foreign terrorist organizations in its annual *Country Reports on Terrorism* (2006, Ch. 8, p. 1)). Still, the *NSCT*'s emphasis on transnational extremists, while reasonable from the standpoint that they are the greatest threat to the

17

US, does so at the expense of not discriminating between the various extremists groups (e.g., irredentist, nationalist, transnational) and their uncommon grievances, a topic this thesis will address in Chapter 5, "Conclusions and Recommendations."

## National Commission

*The 9/11 Commission Report: Final Report of the National Commission on Terrorist Attacks Upon the United States* identified numerous sources of Islamic extremism. Due to the Commission's focus on the 11 September 2001 attacks, much of their analysis specifically addresses al-Qaida's views and grievances against the West.

The Commission asked the question, "Who is this enemy?" (2004, 2). In trying to answer this fundamental question, the Commission looked at Islamic extremism from a historical point of view, but also from the point of view of modern-day extremist leaders such as Usama bin Laden. What they found was an exhaustive list of Muslim and extremist grievances against the West and the US.

The sources of Islamic extremism identified in *The 9/11 Commission Report* cover historical, national, international, and ideological grievances and issues. Specifically, the report's list included: a radical ideology of intolerance motivated by religion that "does not distinguish politics from religion, thus distorting both" (2004, 362); US aggression against Muslims; political and economic malaise in the Middle East; US troops in Saudi Arabia; US policies in the Middle East; change associated with modernization and globalization; suffering of the Iraqi people as a result of sanctions after the 1991 Gulf War; US support of Israel; the decline from Islam's golden age--the caliphate; impious (apostate) and secular Muslim governments; conflicts in the world involving Muslims (e.g., Palestinians, Chechnya, Kashmir, and the southern Philippines);

18

US support of repressive rulers in the Middle East; anticolonial grievances; the 1979

Iranian Revolution; the Afghan jihad against the Soviets from 1979 to 1989; Saudi

Arabia's oil wealth and subsequent promotion of its strict Sunni fundamentalist

interpretation of Wahhabi Islam; and the confluence of Afghan refugees in Pakistan due

to fighting in Afghanistan, a badly strained Pakistani education system, and the growth of

Wahhabism influence nurtured by Saudi-funded institutions.

The report also concluded the enemy is twofold: terrorist networks that must be

dismantled--killed, captured, and denied safe haven; and an extremist ideology that must

be countered for success in the long term.

> The enemy is not Islam, the great world faith, but a perversion of Islam. The enemy goes beyond al Qaeda to include the radical ideological movement, inspired in part by al Qaeda that has spawned other terrorist groups and violence. Thus our strategy must match our two ends: dismantling the al Qaeda network and, in the long term, prevailing over the ideology that contributes to Islamist terrorism. (2004, 16-17)

Lastly, the report makes an important point regarding a global strategy to defeat

Islamic extremism. Long-term success in the global war on terror requires the balanced

use of all elements of national power; over reliance on one element weakens the overall

effort.

> The first phase of our post 9/11 efforts rightly included military action to topple the Taliban and pursue al Qaeda. This work continues. But long-term success demands use of all elements of national power: diplomacy, intelligence, covert action, law enforcement, economic policy, foreign aid, public diplomacy, and homeland defense. If we favor one tool while neglecting others, we leave ourselves vulnerable and weaken our national effort. (2004, 17)

National Intelligence Council

In April 2006, the US government published the classified National Intelligence

Estimate (NIE) titled, *Trends in Global Terrorism: Implications for the United States.* In

September 2006, the Director of National Intelligence (DNI) released the declassified key judgments of the NIE. This thesis addresses only those portions of the NIE that were declassified and released to the public in September 2006. The estimate identified four underlying factors fueling the spread of the "jihadist" movement (note: Islamic extremists often identify themselves as jihadists).

> Four underlying factors are fueling the spread of the jihadist movement: (1) Entrenched grievances, such as corruption, injustice, and fear of Western domination, leading to anger, humiliation, and a sense of powerlessness; (2) the Iraq "jihad;" (3) the slow pace of real and sustained economic, social, and political reforms in many Muslim majority nations; and (4) pervasive anti-US sentiment among most Muslims – all of which jihadists exploit. (2006, 2)

The estimate assesses that the Iraq war is shaping a new generation of extremists and that the extremists' success in Iraq would inspire them to fight elsewhere.

> The Iraq conflict has become the "cause celebre" [incident that attracts great public attention] for jihadists, breeding a deep resentment of US involvement in the Muslim world and cultivating supporters for the global jihadist movement. Should jihadists leaving Iraq perceive themselves, and be perceived, to have failed, we judge fewer fighters will be inspired to carry on the fight. (2006, 2)

Finally, the NIE judges that the number of extremists, while a small percentage of Muslims, is increasing in number and dispersion. The estimate states, "If this trend continues, threats to US interests at home and abroad will become more diverse, leading to increasing attacks worldwide" (2006, 2). This judgment supports the conclusion that understanding the sources of Islamic extremism and designing a strategy to counter them is critical to turning the tide of mainstream Muslims from extremism to moderation.

US Department of State

The State Department's annual *Country Reports on Terrorism* provides a detailed summary of the activities, locations, and strengths of foreign terrorist organizations, other groups of concern, and developments in countries where acts of terrorism have occurred.

The report's strategic assessment focuses primarily on al-Qaida and its associated networks. The assessment notes three sources of Islamic extremism: ideological and propaganda activity, the Iraq war, and the Internet.

First, the report cites indications in 2005 of, "An increasing al-Qaida emphasis on ideological and propaganda activity to help its cause. This led to cooperation between al-Qaida in Iraq, the organization led by Abu Musab al-Zarqawi [note: coalition forces killed Zarqawi in Iraq in June 2006], and with al-Qaida affiliates around the globe, as well as with a new generation of Sunni extremists" (2006, Ch. 2, p. 1).

Second, regarding Iraq and the broader war on terrorism, the report states, "Iraq remains a key front in the global war on terror. . . . Al-Qaida's senior leaders have fully supported the Iraq terrorist movements and see it both as a means to influence and radicalize Muslim public opinion worldwide and as a magnet to draw in as many recruits as possible" (2006, Ch. 2, p. 2).

Lastly, the report describes how al-Qaida has transitioned from a structured network to a diffuse network of like-minded individuals since the loss of their sanctuary base in Afghanistan after 11 September 2001. As a result, some individuals in this new generation of extremists have become, "radicalized 'virtually,' meeting in cyberspace and gaining their training and expertise in part from what they glean from the Internet" (2006, Ch. 2, p. 2).

US Department of Defense

The *National Military Strategic Plan for the War on Terrorism (NMSP-WOT)* constitutes the comprehensive military plan to prosecute the GWOT for the Armed Forces of the US (2006, 3). The *NMSP-WOT* describes how the extremist ideology is the primary source of Islamic extremism. The strategy also compares today's ideological struggle against extremism to the fight against fascist totalitarianism during World War II and against communism during the Cold War. In both of those struggles, the US used all elements of national power (diplomatic, informational, military, and economic) and used coalition partners "to ensure that respect for individual rights and tolerance prevailed over extremism and intolerance" (2006, 11).

Secretary of Defense Rumsfeld, in his introduction letter to the *NMSP-WOT,* states, "Success in this war depends on a strategic offensive and efforts to counter extremist ideologies that fuel terrorism" (2006, 1). Further, the strategy contends that supporting mainstream Muslim efforts to reject violent extremism is a key element of the US government GWOT strategy.

The *NMSP-WOT* makes an important distinction between the sources of extremism for groups like al-Qaida and sources for potential extremist recruits and supporters. The following excerpt from the *NMSP-WOT* argues that for al-Qaida, the source of their extremism is an anti-Western worldview and a desire to establish a pan-Islamic state.

> At the furthest end of the spectrum, some extremists espouse a global insurgency aimed at subverting the existing political order of both the world of Islam and the broader world. They aim to undermine Western influence, redefine the global balance of power, and establish a global pan-Islamist caliphate. Rather than simply seeking to overthrow a particular government in the traditional sense

of the term insurgency, these extremists aim to fundamentally change the nature of the world order. (2006, 18)

For some mainstream Muslims caught in the middle of the struggle between moderation and tolerance on the one hand and extremism and intolerance on the other, the extremist ideology espoused by groups like al-Qaida, tips the balance toward extremism.

> Extremist ideology motivates violent action and inspires individuals to provide material resources. Ideology is the component most critical to extremist networks and movements and sustains all other capabilities. This critical resource is the enemy's center of gravity, and removing it is the key to creating a global antiterrorist environment.
> It is ideological belief, reinforced by propaganda operations, that convinces recruits and supporters that their actions are morally justified. (2006, 11)

The *NMSP-WOT* focuses on the extremists' ideology because it is viewed as the primary vehicle used by extremist organizations to attract new recruits; ideology and propaganda are the foundation for extremist recruiting and indoctrination. Further, the strategy contends that extremist movements can make new terrorists faster than they are killed or captured. For a counterterrorism campaign to be successful, it must attack the extremist ideology by supporting mainstream Muslim efforts to reject extremism.

## International Organizations

### United Nations General Assembly

In September 2006, the UN General Assembly adopted a global counterterrorism strategy resolution, marking the first time that all member states agreed to a common strategic and operational approach to fighting terrorism (UN, *Counter-Terrorism Committee Executive Directorate Fact Sheet*, 2006, 3).

The UN resolution includes a section titled, "Measures to address the conditions conducive to the spread of terrorism." The following excerpt from the resolution highlights those conditions, which include: unresolved conflicts, lack of rule of law, violations of human rights, discrimination, political exclusion, and socioeconomic alienation.

> We resolve to undertake the following measures aimed at addressing the conditions conducive to the spread of terrorism, including but not limited to prolonged unresolved conflicts, dehumanization of victims of terrorism in all its forms and manifestations, lack of the rule of law and violations of human rights, ethnic, national and religious discrimination, political exclusion, socio-economic marginalization and lack of good governance, while recognizing that none of these conditions can excuse or justify acts of terrorism. (UN, *Resolution 60/288*, 2006, 4)

United Nations Alliance of Civilizations Group

The UN's AOC is another international group that has analyzed the sources of Islamic extremism. After the Madrid train bombings in 2004, Spanish Prime Minister Zapatero proposed the AOC group at the UN 59th General Assembly and Turkish Prime Minister Erdogan was named the cosponsor. The AOC initiative analyzed the rise in cross-cultural polarization and extremism and made recommendations on how to counter these issues. To guide this effort, the UN Secretary-General assembled a High-level Group of 20 individuals drawn internationally from policy-making, academia, civil society, religious leadership, and the media.

The High-Level Group's November 2006 report highlighted three principal areas responsible for the present tensions between Western and Muslim societies. These areas include: globalization, Western policies affecting Muslim countries, and trends in Muslim societies. Regarding globalization, the report states:

Aspects of globalization have been experienced by many communities as an assault. For them, the prospect of greater well-being has come at a high price, which includes cultural homogenization, family dislocation, challenges to traditional lifestyles, and environmental degradation. (UN 2006, Highlights p. 1)

The report also contends neither history nor religious differences are responsible for the present tensions. Rather, it argues the root cause lies in political developments-- Western policies and Muslim trends, a topic this thesis will return to in Chapter 5, "Conclusions and Recommendation." The report then breaks the Western policies further into three areas: the Israeli-Palestinian issue, Western military operations in Muslim countries, and the perception of a double standard in the application of international law. Trends in Muslim societies identified by the group include: an internal debate between progressive and regressive forces, interpretations of Islamic teachings, and political repression.

Western policies affecting Muslim countries.
- The Israeli-Palestinian issue has become a key symbol of the rift between Western and Muslim societies and remains one of the gravest threats to international stability.
- Western military operations in Muslim countries contribute to a growing climate of fear and animosity that is spreading around the globe. The spiraling death toll in Iraq and the ongoing conflict in Afghanistan help swell the ranks of terrorist groups.
- Moreover, the perception of double standards in the application of international law and the protection of human rights is increasing resentment and the sense of vulnerability felt by many Muslims around the globe.

Trends in Muslim societies.
- The current predicament from which much of the Muslim world suffers cannot be attributed solely to foreign interference. An internal debate between progressive and regressive forces is playing out on a range of social and political issues throughout the Muslim world as well as on interpretations of Islamic law and traditions, generating deep divisions and, in some cases, leading to extremism and violence.
- In many cases, self-proclaimed religious figures have capitalized on a popular desire for religious guidance to advocate narrow, distorted

interpretations of Islamic teachings. Such figures mis-portray certain cultural traditions, such as honor killings, corporal punishment, and suppression of women to make them appear as religious requirements.

- Resistance to reform and political repression have combined to deprive many Muslim countries of the impetus, hope, and energy needed to achieve economic and social progress. (UN 2006, Highlights p. 1-2)

Lastly, the AOC group makes several recommendations to address the sources of Islamic extremism. Among their recommendations are: reinvigorating the Middle East peace process to reach a settlement to the Israeli-Palestinian issue, facilitating political participation of nonviolent political movements in the Muslim world, training in intercultural understanding for journalists, reviewing educational materials, and developing media campaigns to combat discrimination (UN 2006, Highlights p. 2-4).

International Crisis Group

The International Crisis Group (Crisis Group), a Brussels-based crisis monitoring group, is an independent, nonprofit, multinational organization, with over 100 staff members on five continents, working to prevent and resolve conflicts. In its March 2005 report, *Understanding Islam*, the Crisis Group identified a number of sources of Islamic extremism and made recommendations on how to address them.

First, the group's report contends that the West needs a discriminating strategy toward *Islamism* (Islamic activism) and its three distinctive types: political, missionary, and *Jihadi* (armed struggle)--as opposed to uniformly viewing all types of Islamists as extremists and therefore threatening to Western interests. Further, the report emphasizes how each type of Islamic activism has different goals and grievances. Political Islamic movements, such as the Muslim Brothers in Egypt and the Justice and Development Party (AKP) in Turkey seek to attain political power at the national level. For missionary

Islamic groups, the overriding purpose is the preservation of the Muslim identity and the Islamic faith. *Jihadis* (extremists) use violence to achieve their ends but for different reasons: *internal jihadi* combat Muslim regimes they consider impious or apostate (e.g., Egypt, Algeria, etc.); *irredentist jihadi* fight to redeem land ruled by non-Muslims or under occupation (e.g., Afghanistan, Chechnya, Kashmir, Mindanao and above all Palestine); and *global jihadi* combat the West, or more specifically the US and its allies (e.g., Israel).

Additionally, the report argues that US policy, the Israeli-Palestinian conflict, the war in Iraq, and the way in which the war against terrorism is being waged all strengthen the appeal of the most virulent and dangerous jihadi tendencies. As the following excerpt from *Understanding Islam* shows, while the war on terrorism is not itself a cause of Islamic extremism, the group's report argues the way it has been conducted exacerbates the problem.

> The "war on terrorism" is by no means the cause of this threat, but the way in which it has been conducted – the attack on and occupation of Iraq, the resort to torture, the blanket stigmatization of all forms of jihad as terrorism, the suspension of Western legal norms in respect of people accused of involvement in terrorism (Guantanamo, Belmarsh) and the absence of serious measures to address the Palestinian question – has clearly exacerbated it. . . . (2005, 25)

The report also identifies the Afghan-Soviet War (1979-1989) and the ideology of al-Qaida as sources of Islamic extremism. The report states that the Afghan-Soviet War had a radicalizing effect in three respects: its intoxicating success in causing the Soviet withdrawal laid the basis for belief that a superpower could be defeated by jihad, it was a life-changing experience for participants who had difficulty reintegrating into their countries of origin, and it facilitated the formation of a network of extremists.

Regarding al-Qaida's ideology, the report argues that it combines some elements of ultratraditional Wahabbism with Ayman al-Zawahiri's Egyptian radicalism resulting in an ideology exhibiting the following features: the reorientation of the traditionalist concept of jihad from an alliance with the West (e.g., Afghan-Soviet War) to direct confrontation with the US; the reorientation of *takfiri* (the act of denouncing something or someone as an infidel) from local Muslim regimes ("the near enemy") to Israel and the US as Israel's sponsor ("the far enemy"); the recycling of the Wahhabi vision of Christians and Jews as infidels to be combated, as opposed to earlier concepts of them being "People of the Book"; and the tactical reorientation from guerilla warfare (e.g., Afghanistan) to urban terrorism.

The Crisis Group report takes a discriminatory approach toward Islamists groups and their respective grievances or sources of extremism. The main sources of Islamic extremism highlighted in the report include: non-Muslim rule in Islamic land, apostate Muslim governments, al-Qaida's ideology, the Israel-Palestinian conflict, the Iraq war, the way in which the war on terrorism is being conducted, the Afghan-Soviet War, and "the suspension of Western legal norms" (2006, 25) for individuals accused of involvement in terrorism.

### Nongovernmental Organizations And Civilian Experts

### RAND Corporation

As mentioned in Chapter 1, "Introduction," in 2004 the RAND Corporation prepared a report for the US Air Force titled *The Muslim World After 9/11* in which they examined the sources of Islamic extremism. The report divided the sources into three classes: conditions, processes, and catalytic events.

First, the report defines conditions as factors that have a permanent or quasi-permanent character. The three conditions identified include: failed political and economic models implemented by repressive, corrupt, and unrepresentative regimes; structural anti-Westernism due to economic and social dislocation associated with failed modernization and the lack of channels to express political dissent; and decentralization of religious authority in Sunni Islam (i.e., the lack of institutional mechanisms within the religious infrastructure to control extremists).

Second, the report defines processes as developments that occur over an extended period of time which can have a particular outcome or equilibrium state. Processes identified include: the Islamic resurgence beginning in the 1970s characterized by greater religiosity (e.g., traditional Islamic dress, greater social distance between sexes, dietary restrictions); the Arabization of the non-Arab Muslim world and the polarizing effect of Arab influence in Southeast Asia against local practices; the external funding of religious fundamentalism and extremism such as Saudi funding and export of the Wahhabi version of Islam; the convergence of Islamism and tribalism (e.g., Saudi-Yemeni border area, southeastern Afghanistan, Baluchistan, and the Federally Administered Tribal Areas (FATA) of Pakistan); the growth of radical Islamic networks such as the social services provided by Hezbollah and Hamas, and health services offered by Saudi foundations in Chechnya, the Balkans, Somalia, Indonesia and other areas of conflict; the emergence of the mass media and "often irresponsible satellite regional media," (2004, 46) such as Al-Jazeera; and the Palestinian-Israeli and Kashmir conflicts which discredit Arab governments and Pakistan in the eyes of their citizens, but are also used by governments to divert discontent with domestic conditions.

29

Third, the report defines catalytic events as major developments--wars or revolutions--that change the political dynamics in a region or country in a fundamental way. Catalytic events identified include: the Iranian revolution which demonstrated fundamentalists could overthrow a secular government supported by the US; the Afghan war which was a rallying cry for extremist recruitment, a training ground for today's Islamic extremists, and a context for the creation of global extremist networks; the Gulf War of 1991 (e.g., US forces in Saudi Arabia); 11 September 2001 and the GWOT (e.g., some mainstream Muslims voice opposition to US operations in Afghanistan and to global counterterrorism operations and criticize their government's support of the US-led war on terror); and the Iraq war owing to the US occupation, civilian casualties, destruction of infrastructure, and delays in reconstruction and restoration of services.

Lastly, the report suggests a number of options to respond to Islamic extremism including: disrupting radical networks and promoting moderate network creation; fostering madrassa and mosque reform; expanding economic opportunities; supporting Muslim civil society that advocates moderation and modernity; denying resources to extremists such as funding from Saudi Arabia and the Persian Gulf; balancing the requirements of the war on terrorism and of stability and democracy in moderate Muslim countries; seeking to engage Islamists in normal politics; engaging Muslim diasporas; rebuilding close military-to-military relations with key countries such as Pakistan, Turkey and Indonesia; and building appropriate military capabilities such as intelligence, psychological operations and civil affairs.

Center for Strategic and International Studies

In 2004, the Center for Strategic and International Studies (CSIS) launched the

Transatlantic Dialogue on Terrorism to promote an open and timely discourse between

counterterrorism experts from the US and Europe on the nature of the threat and the root

causes of terrorism.

In August 2004, the Transatlantic Dialogue on Terrorism group released its *Initial*

*Findings* report and identified several sources of Islamic extremism including: ideology,

US policy in the Middle East, and the war in Iraq.  The group also identified four

contributing factors including: poverty, Muslim NGOs, demographics, and the

radicalization of education.

First, the report contends that the extremist ideological nature of the threat is one

of its most dangerous aspects. As the following excerpt from the report indicates, the

ideology has both historical and contemporary roots.

> Radical Islamist violence is a phenomenon driven in part by global
> religious revival. The ideology that animates these terrorists has a number of
> historical roots – in, for example, the reaction to colonialism in the early 20th
> century; the writings of such figures as Maududi and Qutb, based on Wahhabit
> [Wahhabism] principles; and the organization of the Muslim Brotherhood in the
> first third of the last century. More recently, the jihadist movements in the 1970s
> and 1980s in Egypt and the experience of the Muslim resistance to the Soviet
> Union in Afghanistan have been formative ones. . . . (2004, 4)

Second, the report argues that two aspects of US policy are exacerbating

conditions that have strengthened the appeal of the extremists' ideology--the war in Iraq

and the lack of a Middle East peace process.

> From the start, jihadists portrayed the war in Iraq as a war against Islam. . .
> [They] argue that instead of improving the living conditions of Muslims, America
> and its allies are only interested in occupying Muslim lands and subjugating their
> inhabitants.

Similarly, Jihadists have exploited America's effective withdrawal from active diplomacy in the Israeli-Palestinian conflict. Experts from both sides of the Atlantic concur that the plight of Palestinians was of little consequence to the jihadists originally, but, recognizing the importance of the issue to the global Muslim community, they have attached themselves to it with great success. . . . (2004, 6)

Third, the report identifies four key factors that contribute to the radicalization of the ideology and the militarization of Islam including: poverty as a catalyst that can steer people toward terrorist activities they may not undertake under better socioeconomic conditions; Muslim NGOs who, in providing social services that the state cannot, serve as a vehicle to spread the extremist ideology to those in need of assistance; demographics (e.g., the confluence of a youth bulge, urban population growth, and resource scarcity in countries like Iraq, Afghanistan, Pakistan and Saudi Arabia); and the radicalization of education, such as in madrassas in Pakistan and in Jemaah Islamiyah (JI)-established schools in Indonesia, Malaysia, Thailand and the Philippines.

The report also suggests five potential remedies for these problems including: increasing US aid to foster good governance and encouraging countries to become coalition partners; supporting the work of international NGOs who could partner with moderate Muslim NGOs; committing to economic programs that invest in training and job creation, promoting entrepreneurship, supporting family planning services and female education, and increasing access to economic opportunity; providing financial assistance and innovative strategies to reform education; and dedicating necessary resources and attention to the Middle East peace process.

Bernard Lewis

Bernard Lewis is the Cleveland E. Dodge Professor of Near Eastern Studies

Emeritus at Princeton University. Lewis is an internationally recognized historian of the

Middle East and his books have been translated into over twenty languages, including

Arabic, Persian, Turkish, and Indonesian.

Lewis's book, *The Crisis of Islam, Holy War and Unholy Terror*, examines the

sources of Islamic extremism from historical and contemporary perspectives. His analysis

covers the 13 centuries of history since the birth of Islam but focuses on contemporary

issues that give rise to terrorism.

Lewis provides the historical context that traces the lines of conflict with Islam to

its two major periods of expansion: during the seventh and eighth centuries under

Mohammed and the reign of his successors or caliphs, and from the fourteenth to

seventeenth centuries under the Ottoman Empire. He notes that even today in the twenty-

first century, conflicts exist along the fault lines that mark the edge of historical Islamic

expansion in areas such as Bosnia and Kosovo, Chechnya, Mindanao in the southern

Philippines, Israel-Palestine, Kashmir, Sudan and Nigeria.

Regarding contemporary issues, Lewis cites the litany of grievances that are

commonly used to explain the sources of Islamic extremism including: Westernization

and what extremists call its "moral degeneracy", globalization, modernization, poverty

and frustration due to the economic disparity between the Muslim world and the West,

apostate Muslim governments and their Western supporters, colonialism and imperialism

such as the exploitation of oil wealth and Western troops in Islamic lands, "The marriage

of Saudi power and Wahhabi teaching," the establishment of the state of Israel and

Western support to Israel against the Palestinians, the defeat in 1989 of Soviets in

Afghanistan and collapse in 1991 of the Soviet Union (note: extremists believe the

former caused the latter), the Gulf War of 1991 and subsequent sanctions against Iraq

(note: Baghdad was the seat of the Islamic caliphate for 500 years). From this list, Lewis

highlights several overarching issues as they relate to contemporary Islamic extremism.

First, Lewis emphasizes that apostate Muslim governments ("tyrannies") are a

source of Islamic extremism. According to extremists, these governments deviate from

the pure Islamic faith and *sharia* (holy law). Therefore, they are traitors and violence

against them is justified because they have known the "true" faith and have abandoned it.

> The Islamic world, in their [extremist] view, has taken a wrong turning. Its rulers
> call themselves Muslims and make a pretense of Islam, but they are in fact
> apostates who have abrogated the Holy Law and adopted foreign and infidel laws
> and customs. The only solution, for them, is a return to the authentic Muslim way
> of life, and for this the removal of apostate governments is an essential first step.
> Fundamentalists are anti-Western in the sense that they regard the West as the
> source of the evil that is corroding Muslim society, but their primary attack is
> directed against their own rulers and leaders. (2004, 24)

Second, Islamic extremists view the US antagonistically because they perceive

the US as being the leader of the West and by extension responsible for Westernization.

> The basic reason is that America is now perceived as the leader of what is
> variously designated as the West, Christendom, or more generally the "Lands of
> the Unbelievers." In this sense the American president is the successor of a long
> line of rulers – the Byzantine emperors of Constantinople, the Holy Roman
> emperors in Vienna, Queen Victoria and her imperial colleagues and successors in
> Europe. Today as in the past, this world of Christian unbelievers is seen as the
> only serious force rivaling and obstructing the divinely ordained spread of Islam,
> resisting and delaying but not preventing its final, inevitable, universal triumph.
> (2004, 160)

Specifically addressing the American way of life, Lewis contends that extremists

see American society as degenerate and demoralized. Furthermore, extremists view the

American way of life as a grave threat to Islam.

34

Today, America exemplifies the civilization of the House of War [*Dar al-Harb* – land ruled by non-Muslims or infidels], and like Rome and Byzantium, it has become degenerate and demoralized, ready to be overthrown. But despite its weakness, it is also dangerous. Khomeini's designation of the United States as "the Great Satan" was telling, and for the members of Al-Qai'da it is the seduction of America and of its profligate, dissolute way of life that represents the greatest threat to the kind of Islam they wish to impose on their fellow Muslims. (2004, 163)

Third, Lewis identifies globalization as a source of Islamic extremism. Poverty affects the majority of the Muslim world and the poor economic condition of most Muslim countries compared to the rest of the world fuels frustration, particularly among unemployed, uneducated men.

The people of the Middle East are increasingly aware of the deep and widening gulf between the opportunities of the free world outside their borders and the appalling privation and repression within them. The resulting anger is naturally directed first against their rulers, and then against those whom they see as keeping those rulers in power for selfish reasons. . . . (2004, 119)

Lastly, Lewis addresses what he calls "the marriage of Saudi power and Wahhabi teaching." He describes Wahhabism as the rejection of modernity in favor of a return to the sacred past. According to Lewis, the declared aim of its founder, Muhammad ibn 'Abd al-Wahhab (1703-1792), was "to return to the pure and authentic Islam of the founder [Muhammed]" (2004, 120).

Further, Lewis contends that the confluence of several factors--Wahhabism, Saudi power, petrodollars and *madrassas* (centers of higher education)--have changed Saudi Arabia's external role and influence in the Muslim world. The following excerpt from *The Crisis of Islam, Holy War and Unholy Terror* ties these four factors together well.

The outward flow of oil and the corresponding inward flow of money brought immense changes to the Saudi kingdom, its internal structure and way of life, and its external role and influence, both in the oil-consuming countries and, more powerfully, in the world of Islam. The most significant change was in the impact of Wahhabism and the role of its protagonists. Wahhabism was now the official, state-enforced doctrine of one of the most influential governments in all of Islam – the custodian of the two holiest places of Islam, the host of the annual pilgrimage, which brings millions of Muslims from every part of the world to share in its rites and rituals. At the same time, the teacher and preachers of Wahhabism had at their disposal immense financial resources, which they used to promote and spread their version of Islam. . . . (2004, 127-128)

John Esposito

John L. Esposito is a University Professor of Religion and International Affairs and the Director of the Prince Alwaleed Bin Talal Center for Muslim-Christian Understanding at Georgetown University. Esposito is also the author of several books on Islam, a member of the UN's AOC group, and is currently working with the Gallup Organization to produce an in-depth study on opinions in the Muslim world.

In his book, *Unholy War: Terror in the Name of Islam,* Esposito seeks to explain the politics of the Muslim world and the sources of Islamic extremism. Highlighting his major points, Esposito contends that the principal sources of Islamic extremism are historical grievances (e.g., the Crusades, European colonialism, the Cold War, American neocolonialism), corrupt authoritarian regimes propped up by Western governments, and contemporary grievances such as US policies in the Middle East. He also discusses Wahabbism and its impact on Islamic extremism.

First, Esposito argues that historical grievances are a source of Islamic extremism and cites the Crusades and the creation of Israel among other grievances.

Many violent radicals justify the horrors they commit by reciting a litany of deeply felt Muslim grievances against the West. Historic memories of the Crusades and European colonialism, the creation of Israel, the Cold War, and American neocolonialism--all actions of a militant Christian West--get superimposed upon current events. . . . (2003, 73)

Second, Esposito contends that authoritarian regimes in the Muslim world and the Western governments that support them are a primary source of Islamic extremism. The

36

West is not simply an antagonist because of its support to authoritarian governments, but also because of the perceived penetration of Western culture into the Muslim world and the perceived exploitation of wealth from Muslim countries.

> Many Muslims today believe that the conditions of their world require a jihad. They look around them and see a world dominated by corrupt authoritarian governments and a wealthy elite, a minority concerned solely with its own economic prosperity, rather than national development, a world awash in Western culture and values in dress, music, television, and movies. Western governments are perceived as propping up oppressive regimes and exploiting the region's human and natural resources, robbing Muslims of their culture and their options to be governed according to their own choice and to live in a more just society. (2003, 27)

Further, Esposito argues that US policies in the war on terror since 11 September 2001 have reversed international sympathy for America and fueled anti-Americanism. The following excerpt from *Unholy War: Terror in the Name of Islam* reflects Esposito's argument of how US policies in Iraq, Israel, and elsewhere have increased anti-Americanism and Islamic extremism.

> Among the key factors were the broadening of the American-led military campaign's scope beyond Afghanistan, talk of second frontiers and in particular the "axis of evil" countries (Syria and Iran), America's continued "pro-Israel" policy during the second intifada in Israel/Palestine and failure to effectively pressure Israel to halt Israeli military action in the West Bank and Gaza, and President Bush's unilateral approach to the war in Iraq. One-sided American rhetoric and policies not only in Israel / Palestine but also India / Pakistan (regarding Kashmir) and Russia / Chechnya also fed anti-American sentiment among mainstream Muslims and hatred of America among militant extremists. (2003, iix-ix)

Esposito also addresses the issue of Wahhabism relative to Islamic extremism. According to Esposito, Wahhabism describes Saudi Arabia's ultraconservative, puritanical brand of Islam which is fueled by petrodollars, produces a number of different Islamist groups, and uses madrassas to export its ideology.

Presenting their version of Islam as the pristine, pure, unadulterated message, the Wahhabi seek to impose their strict beliefs and interpretations, which are not commonly shared by other Sunni or by Shia Muslims throughout the Muslim world. . . .

The Wahhabi vision went international in the 1960s in response to the threat posed by Arab nationalism and socialism. It was fueled by petrodollars, especially from skyrocketing revenues after the 1973 oil embargo. . . .
. . . . . . . . . . . . . . . . . . . . . . . . . . . . . . . . . . . . . . . . . . . . . . . . . . . . . . . . .
Saudi initiatives produced a rapid growth of Islamist groups and the dissemination of their worldview and fundamentalist interpretations of Islam in many countries. . . .
. . . . . . . . . . . . . . . .
Pakistan's madrassa system has for many decades enjoyed substantial funding from Saudi Arabia and the Gulf, an important reason why the number of madrassas in Pakistan has grown from 147 in 1947 to more than 9,000 today. . . . (2003, 106, 108-109)

Lastly, Esposito makes several recommendations on how to counter Islamic extremism including: reassessing foreign policies and support for authoritarian regimes, increasing the capacity of mainstream Muslims to address religious extremism, reforming the training of religious scholars and leaders, discrediting militant jihadist ideas and ideologies, and balancing nonmilitary components of any counterterrorism strategy to address the political and economic causes of global terrorism.

## Islamic Extremists

Whereas many of the sources of Islamic extremism for moderate Muslims are political or economic in nature, the sources of extremism for extremists themselves are principally religious or ideological in nature. For example, in a May 1998 interview with ABC news, Usama bin Laden articulated his view that the current conflict between the Muslim world and the West is religious in nature.

All people who worship Allah, not each other, are equal before Him. We are entrusted to spread this message and to extend that call to all the people. We, nonetheless, fight against their governments and all those who approve of the

38

injustice they practice against us. We fight the governments that are bent on attacking our religion and stealing our wealth. . . . (1998, 3-4)

While there are certainly ideological differences among Islamic extremists (which moderates and the West should seek to exploit), the writings and teachings of historical and contemporary Islamic extremist ideologues, such as Taqi ad-Din Ahmed ibn Taymiyya (1263-1328), Hassan al-Banna (1906-1949), Sayyid Qutb (1906-1966) and Usama bin Laden (1957-) are similar in that they reflect an intolerant ideological worldview whose dogma puts them at odds with moderate Muslims and the West.

Principal tenets of their ideology include: the rejection of all other systems (e.g., democracy, liberalism, communism, socialism, etc.) that are not based on the Quran, the *Sunnah* (deeds and words of the Prophet) and the *Hadith* (traditions of the Prophet); the imposition of absolute sharia law; the legitimacy of offensive and defensive jihad against *kafir* (infidels); the use of violence against "apostate" Muslim governments; and the concept of *takfir* (to excommunicate or declare as unbelievers) whereby extremists legitimize violence against Muslims who do not agree with their version of Islam. Additionally, some extremist ideologues like bin Laden desire a return to the *caliphate* (pan-Islamic state) like that of the seventh century under Mohammed's successors.

### Taqi ad-Din Ahmed Ibn Taymiyya (1263-1328)

Contemporary Islamic extremists often refer to Ibn Taymiyya, born in present-day Turkey near the Syrian border, in their arguments against what they consider "apostate" Muslim governments. Taymiyya moved to Damascus to escape the Mongol invasion from the east and the historical context of his teaching is one where the Mongols had invaded the Muslim world; their king converted to Islam, but maintained some aspects of

Mongol law versus implementing absolute sharia law. Because the Muslim Mongol rulers did not adopt pure sharia law, Taymiyya argued they were acting contrary to the Quranic text and therefore jihad against them was required (Habeck 2006, 19).

> Ibn Taymiyya needed an argument that would rally Muslims behind the Mamluke rulers and their struggle against the advancing Mongols from 1294 to 1303. Some objected that there could be no jihad against the Mongols because they and their king had recently converted to Islam. Ibn Taymiyya reasoned that because the Mongol ruler permitted some aspects of Mongol tribal law to persist alongside the Islamic *sharia* code, the Mongols were apostates to Islam and therefore legitimate targets of jihad. (Henzel 2005, 2)

Taymiyya is also significant because of his theories on jihad--he argued that it applied not only to infidels but also to Muslims who did not participate in jihad. Mary Habeck's book, *Knowing the Enemy: Jihadist Ideology and the War on Terror,* is an excellent resource on extremist ideology and the historical context of extremist ideologues such as Taymiyya. The following excerpt from Habeck's book captures Taymiyya's theory about jihad.

> Ibn Taymiyya also broadened the definition of jihadic activity, creating one of the first serious reconsiderations of the obligation since the time of Muhammed. After a careful study of the relevant traditions and Qur'anic passages, he concluded that not only should the Islamic nation fight all heretics, apostates, hypocrites, sinners, and unbelievers (including Christians and Jews) until 'all religion was for God alone,' but also any Muslim who tried to avoid participating in jihad. . . . (Habeck 2006, 21)

Taymiyya died in confinement in Damascus and his teachings fell into relative obscurity until the nineteenth century and the beginning of the twentieth century when a number of events in the Muslim world led to a revival of the Islamic extremist ideology. First, in 1798 Napoleon conquered Egypt--the first time a Western power had dominated a piece of land in the heart of the Muslim world since the Crusades. Second, after World War I most of the Muslim world fell under European rule. Both of these events resulted in imperialism and Westernization in the Muslim world coinciding with a decline in Muslim power. Two Egyptian Islamic extremist ideologues who spoke out against these developments were Hassan Al-Banna and Sayyid Qutb (Habeck 2006, 26-29).

## Hassan Al-Banna (1906-1949)

Hassan Al-Banna was born in Egypt in 1906 and in 1928 he founded an Islamic ideological party, the Muslim Brotherhood. Al-Banna sought to unite and mobilize Muslims against cultural and political domination by the West as well as against secular Muslim regimes, especially in Egypt. As the following quote from Al-Banna indicates, he believed that the West was an intellectual and physical threat to Islam and that jihad was required first in Egypt, but then in the rest of the world.

> Our task in general is to stand against the flood of modernist civilization overflowing from the swamp of materialistic and sinful desires. This flood has swept the Muslim nation away from the Prophet's leadership and Qur'anic guidance and deprived the world of its guiding light. Western secularism moved into a Muslim world already estranged from its Qur'anic roots, and delayed its advancement for centuries, and will continue to do so until we drive it from our lands. Moreover, we will not stop at this point, but will pursue this evil force to its own lands, invade its Western heartland, and struggle to overcome it until all the world shouts by the name of the Prophet and the teachings of Islam spread throughout the world. . . . (Al-Banna quoted in Habeck 2006, 31-32)

Al-Banna was not solely intent on jihad for the purpose of killing unbelievers. Rather, he believed Muslims were appointed to save humanity and lead them to the one true path of Islam.

> Al-Banna argued that the eventual resort to violence would not be to avenge wrongs suffered, nor to kill unbelievers, but to save humankind from its many problems. The Qur'an had appointed Muslims as guardians over humanity and given them the right to dominion over the world, but only so that they could guide people to the truth, lead mankind to the good, and illuminate the whole world with the "sun of Islam." Jihad was then a social duty God had delegated to Muslims so that they would become an "army of salvation" to rescue humanity and lead them all together on one path. (Habeck 2006, 32-33)

Al-Banna was killed by Egyptian police in February 1949 after a member of the Muslim brotherhood assassinated the Egyptian Prime Minister in December 1948.

## Sayyid Qutb (1906-1966)

Like Al-Banna, Sayyid Qutb was born in Egypt in 1906. Influenced by Al-Banna and also a member of the Muslim Brotherhood, Qutb was a prolific ideological writer and his books *In the Shade of the Qur'an* and *Milestones* provide much of the foundation for contemporary Islamic extremist philosophy. Three ideas stand at the heart of Qutb's extremist ideology including: advocating pure *sharia* (servitude to God) against any system where there exists a separation of church and state, which he equated to servitude to man; articulating the concept of *Islam* (submission to God) versus *jayiliyya* (living in ignorance of God); and arguing for the legitimacy of jihad against "apostate" Muslim governments (tyranny) and against those who did not heed the call to "true" Islam; his vision of Islam.

First, Qutb argued that because the Quran comes from God, it was superior to all other legal systems. Further, Qutb believed that sharia resulted in man's servitude to God, while adherence to any other legal system meant servitude to something other than God such as other men. For Muslims to follow the "true" path, the acceptance of sharia must be absolute.

> The love of the Divine Law *al-Sari'ah* should be a consequence of pure submission to God and of freedom from servitude to anyone else, and not because it is superior to other systems in such and such details. . . . The basis of the message is that one should accept the *Shari'ah* without any question and reject all other laws in any shape or form. This is Islam. (1964, 36)

Second, Qutb argued that being a "true" Muslim meant complete submission to God and its law (*sharia*); all others were *jayiliyya*.

The *jahili* society is any society other than the Muslim society; and if we want a more specific definition, we may say that any society is a *jahili* society which does not dedicate itself to submission to God alone, in its beliefs and ideas, in its observances of worship, and in its legal regulations. According to this definition, all the societies existing in the world today are *jahili*. (1964, 80)

Most significantly, Qutb argued that not only were non-Muslims inherently jayiliyya but because Muslim states had deviated from pure sharia and the "true" path of Islam, they also were jayiliyya. Therefore, Qutb argued the entire world was in a state of jayiliyya.

Lastly, all the existing so-called 'Muslim' societies are also *jahili* societies.

We classify them among *jahili* societies not because they believe in other deities besides God or because they worship anyone other than God, but because their way of life is not based on submission to God alone. Although they believe in the Unity of God, still they have relegated the legislative attribute of God to others and submit to this authority, and from this authority they derive their systems, their traditions and customs, their laws, their values and standards, and almost every practice of life. . . . (1964, 82)

Third, Qutb combined the concepts of sharia, jahiliyya and jihad and argued that jihad against "apostate" Muslim governments (tyrannies) and those Muslims who did not heed the call to "true" Islam was required. He believed jihad was intended to free men from servitude to other men where men followed laws other than the divinely based sharia.

The Jihaad of Islam is to secure complete freedom for every man throughout the world by releasing him from servitude to other human beings so that he may serve his God, Who is One and Who has no associates. . . . (1964, 70)

Finally, Qutb also argued that jihad would be intellectual and physical--preaching ideas as well as fighting.

This movement uses the methods of preaching and persuasion for reforming ideas and beliefs; it uses physical power and *Jihaad* for abolishing the organizations

43

and authorities of the *Jahili* system which prevents people from reforming their ideas and beliefs but forces them to obey their erroneous ways and make them serve human lords instead of the Almighty Lord. . . . (1964, 55)

Qutb was hanged in 1966 for plotting against the Egyptian government but his philosophies would influence the next generation of Islamic extremists including fellow Egyptian Ayman al-Zawahiri (1951-) and Saudi Usama bin Laden (1957-). However, whereas Al-Banna's and Qutb's animosity toward "apostate" rulers and the West was primarily due to secularism in the Muslim world and European domination, Zawahiri and bin Laden were further radicalized by the Israeli-Palestinian conflict, the Afghan-Soviet war, and the presence of US troops in Saudi Arabia.

## Usama bin Laden (1957--)

Usama bin Laden, the founder of al-Qaida, has identified his grievances through audio and video tapes, statements released to the media and through interviews. Bruce Lawrence's (editor) and James Howarth's (translator) 2005 detailed translation and analysis of bin Laden's statements is an excellent source of information on bin Laden's grievances and ideology.

To understand the context of his extremist ideology, several biographical points require highlighting. Bin Laden was the seventeenth of fifty-seven children of Muhammed bin Laden, a construction magnate, who died in a 1968 helicopter crash leaving a multibillion dollar fortune to his children (The 9/11 Commission Report 2004, 55) (note: the number of bin Laden siblings varies depending on the source, but the number is generally accepted to be in the 50-range). In a 1996 interview in *Nida'ul Islam*, a journal edited by Muslim activists in Australia, bin Laden dates his own radicalization to 1973, the year of the Yom Kippur War (Lawrence 2005, 31). In 1980, he arrived in

44

Peshawar, Pakistan near the Afghanistan border to organize the flow of funds and equipment to the *mujahedeen* (one who participates in jihad) who had taken up arms against the Soviet Union and the Soviet-backed Afghan government; he subsequently founded *al-Qaida* (the base). After the Soviet withdrawal from Afghanistan in 1989, bin Laden returned to Saudi Arabia and was critical of the Saudi government for allowing the basing of US troops in Saudi Arabia. After Saudi authorities placed him under house arrest, bin Laden left for Sudan in 1991. Saudi Arabia revoked his citizenship in 1994. With the Sudanese government under pressure to expel him, bin Laden returned to Afghanistan in May 1996. In August 1996, he issued a fatwa, *Declaration of War against the Americans Occupying the Land of the Two Holy Places*, a reference to the US troop presence in Saudi Arabia and to Saudi Arabia's two holiest sites--Mecca and Medina. In September 1996, the Taliban captured Kabul and eventually the majority of Afghanistan--bin Laden now had a safe haven from which to organize fighters for the defense of Islam (Lawrence 2005, xi-xv).

Bin Laden's statements indicate that he views the reasons for the current conflict as a continuation of a historical struggle or "Crusade" by the West against Islam. In November 2001, al-Jazeera transmitted a bin Laden statement where he argued that the US's 2001 attack on Afghanistan was only the latest in a long series of aggression against Islam dating back to the division of the Islamic world by European powers after World War I.

> Look at this war that began some days ago against Afghanistan. Is it a single unrelated event, or is it part of a long series of Crusader wars against the Islamic world? Since World War One, which ended over 83 years ago, the entire Islamic world has fallen under the Crusader banners, under the British, French, and Italian governments. They divided up the whole world between them, and Palestine fell

into the hands of the British. From that day to this, more than 83 years later, our brothers and sons have been tortured in Palestine. (Bin Laden 2001)

Turning to his contemporary grievances, Bin Laden's 2002 letter *To the Americans* provides a synopsis of his ideology and the reasons behind Islamic extremists' attacks. Chief among these are the following US offenses: attacks against Muslims, support to "apostate" Muslim governments, the "theft" of Muslim oil, the presence of US troops in the Muslim world, sanctions against Iraq after the 1991 Gulf War, and support to Israel. The following excerpt from bin Laden's letter identifies seven reasons why extremists are fighting the US and seven things that bin Laden "wants Americans to do" (note: only the letter's section headings are listed below).

Why are we fighting and opposing you? Because you attacked us and continue to attack us.

(1) You attacked us in Palestine.
(2) You attacked us in Somalia; you supported the Russian atrocities against us in Chechnya, the Indian oppression against us in Kashmir, and the Jewish aggression against us in Lebanon.
(3) Under your supervision, consent, and orders, the governments of our countries which act as your collaborators, attack us on a daily basis.
(4) You steal our wealth and oil at paltry prices because of your international influence and military threats. This theft is indeed the biggest theft ever witnessed by mankind in the history of the world.
(5) Your forces occupy our countries; you spread your military bases throughout them; you corrupt our lands, and you besiege our sanctuaries.
(6) You have starved the Muslims of Iraq, where children die every day. It is a wonder that more than 1.5 million Iraqi children have died as a result of your sanctions, and that you have not shown concern. Yet when 3,000 of your people died, the entire world rises up and has not yet sat down.
(7) You have supported the Jews in their idea that Jerusalem is their eternal capital, and you have agreed to move your embassy there. With your help and under your protection, the Israelis are planning to destroy the al-Aqsa mosque. Under the protection of your weapons, Sharon entered the al-Aqsa mosque, to pollute it as a preparation to capture and destroy it.

As for the second question that we want to answer: What are we calling you to, and what do we want from you?

46

(1) The first thing that we are calling you to is Islam.

(2) The second thing we call you to, is to stop your oppression, lies, immorality, and debauchery that has spread among you.

(3) What we call you to thirdly is to take an honest stance with yourselves – and I doubt you will do so – in order to discover that you are a nation without principles or manners, and that, to you, values and principles are something which you must demand from others, not that which you yourself must adhere.

(4) We also advise you to stop supporting Israel, and to end your support of the Indians in Kashmir, the Russians against the Chechens, and also to cease supporting the Manila Government against the Muslims in the southern Philippines.

(5) We also advise you to pack your luggage and get out of our lands. We only desire this for your goodness, guidance, and righteousness, so do not force us to send you back as cargo in coffins.

(6) Sixthly, we call upon you to end your support of the corrupt leaders in our countries. Do not interfere in our politics and method of education. Leave us alone, or else expect us in New York and Washington.

(7) We also call you to deal with us and interact with us on the basis of mutual interests and benefits, rather than the policies of subjugation, theft, and occupation, and not to continue your policy of supporting the Jews because this will result in more disasters for you. (Bin Laden 2002)

<u>Summary and Conclusions</u>

This thesis seeks to answer the primary research question, Has the *NSS* properly identified the sources of Islamic extremism? In order to answer the primary question, this thesis uses secondary research questions to consider the perspectives of different groups and what they identify as the sources of Islamic extremism. Secondary research questions include: What do the *NSS* and other US government documents identify as the sources of Islamic extremism? What do international organizations identify as the sources of Islamic extremism? What do NGOs and civilian experts identify as the sources of Islamic extremism? What do Islamic extremists identify as the sources of their grievances?

This chapter presented what has been written on the subject by the various groups and highlighted what each group identifies as the sources of Islamic extremism. Chapter

4, "Analysis," will consider the research findings from Chapter 3, "Literature Review," and present what the study found by answering the primary and secondary research questions.

# CHAPTER 4

# ANALYSIS

> Today we are engaged in a critical struggle in a dangerous and uncertain strategic environment. We are facing enemies that endanger our freedoms and our way of life. The stakes are high. The range of dangerous possibilities that exist today has never been more broad or perilous. . . . I do not believe the average American even mildly comprehends the degree to which our nation is in peril, nor does he understand how our way of life is threatened. (2006, 1)
>
> Gen. Peter J. Schoomaker, Speech to Union League of Philadelphia

## Introduction

The purpose of this thesis is to: conduct a qualitative analysis of the sources of Islamic extremism from multiple perspectives, determine if the *NSS* properly identifies the sources of Islamic extremism, and make recommendations on how to counter sources of Islamic extremism and improve US security and counterterrorism strategy.

This chapter analyzes the sources of Islamic extremism based on the "Research Methodology" established in Chapter 2 and the information from the "Literature Review" presented in Chapter 3 in order to answer the primary and secondary research questions listed below:

Primary Research Question: Has the *NSS* properly identified the sources of Islamic extremism?

Secondary Research Questions:

1. What do the *NSS* and other US government documents identify as the sources of Islamic extremism?

2. What do international organizations identify as the sources of Islamic extremism?

3. What do NGOs and civilian experts identify as the sources of Islamic extremism?

4. What do Islamic extremists identify as the sources of their grievances?

This chapter is organized into four parts: introduction, secondary research questions, primary research question, and summary and conclusions.

## Secondary Research Questions

In order to answer the primary research question, four secondary research questions were generated. These questions correlate to the four perspectives researched and to what each group identifies as the sources of Islamic extremism. When answered, these questions are intended to provide the foundation of data necessary to answer the primary research question.

### Secondary Research Question #1 (US Government)

The first secondary research question is, What do the *NSS* and other US government documents identify as the sources of Islamic extremism?

The *NSS* identifies the sources of Islamic extremism as political alienation, grievances that can be blamed on others, subcultures of conspiracy and misinformation, and an ideology that justifies murder--all of which give rise to acts of terrorism. Additionally, the *NSS* contends that terrorism used by Islamic extremists is not the inevitable by-product of poverty, not simply a result of hostility to US policy in Iraq, not simply a response to our efforts to prevent terror attacks, and not simply a result of Israeli-Palestinian issues.

Other US government documents used for this research were the *National Strategy for Combating Terrorism (NSCT)*, *The 9/11 Commission Report*, the National Intelligence Estimate (NIE) *Trends in Global Terrorism*, the Department of State's *2005 Country Reports on Terrorism*, and the Department of Defense's *National Military Strategic Plan for the War on Terrorism (NMSP-WOT)*. US government documents identify five principal sources of Islamic extremism: historical grievances, ideology, globalization, "apostate" or authoritarian Muslim governments, and non-Muslim rule or military presence in Islamic lands. Additionally, *The 9/11 Commission Report* is unique among government sources in that it also identifies Saudi funding of Wahhabi doctrine and US policies as sources of Islamic extremism.

*The 9/11 Commission Report*, the *NSCT* and the *NMSP-WOT* all identify historical grievances as a source of Islamic extremism. Chief among historical grievances cited is a desire by some Islamic extremists to return to the historical caliphate--the institutionalized leadership of the *umma* (community of Islamic believers)--whose territory during the seventh and eighth centuries and later under the Ottoman Empire during the seventeenth century extended from the Middle East to North Africa, Europe and parts of Asia. *The 9/11 Commission Report* describes how the caliphate was disestablished in Turkey in 1924 and how, "Nostalgia for Islam's past glory remains a powerful force." Further, *The 9/11 Commission Report* contends that, "The extreme Islamist version of history blames the decline from Islam's golden age on the rulers and people who turned away from the true path of their religion, thereby leaving Islam vulnerable to encroaching foreign powers eager to steal their land, wealth, and even their souls" (2004, 50). The *NSCT* describes how Islamic extremists desire a return to the historical caliphate when it says, "Some among the enemy, particularly al-Qaida, harbor even greater territorial and geopolitical ambitions and aim to establish a single, pan-Islamic, totalitarian regime that stretches from Spain to Southeast Asia" (2006, 5). Lastly, the *NMSP-WOT* states that some extremists "aim to undermine Western influence, redefine the global balance of power, and establish a global pan-Islamic caliphate" (2006, 11).

US government documents were unanimous in identifying the extremist ideology as a source of Islamic extremism. In describing today's terrorist enemy, the *NSCT* states that the extremists' ideology of oppression, violence and hate unites the movement (2006, 5). *The 9/11 Commission Report* calls the extremists' ideology one of extreme intolerance within one stream of Islam (a minority tradition) that "is motivated by religion and does not distinguish politics from religion, thus distorting both" (2004, 362). The State Department reports that in 2005 it saw an increasing al-Qaida emphasis on ideological and propaganda activity to help advance its cause (2006, Ch. 2, p. 1). Significantly, the NIE notes the limited appeal of the extremist ideology among the vast majority of Muslims and contends that its ultraconservative interpretation of sharia-based governance is the extremists' greatest vulnerability (2006, 2).

US government sources also were unanimous in identifying globalization or westernization as a source of Islamic extremism. The *NSCT* describes how extremists believe the US is the cause of most problems affecting Muslims today and how they seek to expel Western power and influence from the Muslim world (2006, 5). *The 9/11 Commission Report* contends that Usama bin Laden's appeal in the Islamic world is that, "He appeals to people disoriented by cyclonic change as they confront modernity and globalization" (2004, 48). The NIE states that anti-US and antiglobalization sentiment is on the rise and fueling other radical ideologies and that radicalization is growing more quickly and anonymously in the Internet age (2006, 3-4). Ironically, while extremists are opposed to the Western (US-led) globalization system, they use the Internet--an element of globalization--to advance their cause. The State Department's report describes how a new generation of extremists have become radicalized 'virtually,' meeting in cyberspace and gaining their training and expertise in part from the Internet (2006, Ch. 2, p. 2).

Several government documents identify "apostate" or authoritarian Muslim governments as a source of Islamic extremism where, because of their perceived secularism or repression, these governments have alienated elements of their population. The *NSCT* conveys how transnational terrorists are recruited from people who have no voice in their government and see no way to promote change in their country (2006, 9). *The 9/11 Commission Report* contends that extremists view Muslim governments as "false Muslims usurping God's authority" because of the existence of parliaments, legislation, and distinctions between church and state (2004, 50). Further, the NIE assesses that one of the underlying factors fueling the spread of Islamic extremism is the slow pace of economic, social, and political reforms in many Muslim majority nations (2006, 2).

Lastly, some US government sources identify non-Muslim rule or western military presence in Islamic lands as a source of Islamic extremism. *The 9/11 Commission Report* states that extremism is fed by grievances widely felt throughout the Muslim world such as the US military presence in the Middle East and support for Israel (2004, 362). The NIE cites the Iraq war as an underlying factor fueling the spread of extremism and states that, "The Iraq conflict has become the 'cause celebre' for jihadists, breeding a deep resentment of US involvement in the Muslim world and cultivating supporters for the global jihadist movement" (2006, 2). The State Department's report says that, "Al-Qaida's senior leaders have fully supported the Iraq terrorist movement and see it both as a means to influence and radicalize Muslim public opinion worldwide and as a magnet to draw in as many recruits as possible" (2006, Ch. 2, p. 2).

Of note, while US policies and Saudi funding of Wahhabi doctrine are frequently identified as sources of Islamic extremism by other perspectives considered in this study, among US government sources only *The 9/11 Commission Report* identifies them as such. The following two excerpts from the commission's report describe Bin Laden's attempts to rally the Muslim world against US polices in the Middle East and the growth in influence of Wahhabi teaching relative to al-Qaida's renewal in Afghanistan in the late-1990s.

> He [Bin Laden] also stresses grievances against the United States widely shared in the Muslim world. He inveighed [protest vehemently] against the presence of US troops in Saudi Arabia, the home of Islam's holiest sites. He spoke of the suffering of the Iraqi people as a result of sanctions imposed after the Gulf War, and he protested US support to Israel.
> . . . . . . . . . . . . .
> The influence of the Wahhabi school of Islam had also grown, nurtured by Saudi-funded institutions. Moreover, the fighting in Afghanistan made Pakistan home to an enormous – and generally unwelcome – population of Afghan refugees; and since the badly strained Pakistani education system could not accommodate the refugees, the government increasingly let privately funded religious schools serve as a cost-free alternative. Over time, these schools produced large numbers of half-educated young men with no marketable skills but with deeply held Islamic views. (2004, 48-49, 63)

Secondary Research Question #2 (International Organizations)

The second secondary research question is, What do international organizations identify as the sources of Islamic extremism? International organizations used for this

54

research were the UN, the AOC group, and the International Crisis Group (Crisis Group).

International organizations identify five principal sources of Islamic extremism: historical

grievances, globalization, "apostate" or authoritarian Muslim governments, non-Muslim

rule or military presence in Islamic lands, and US policies.

The AOC group and the Crisis Group identify historical grievances as a source of

Islamic extremism. The AOC group cites European imperialism and the resulting

anticolonial movement during the nineteenth and twentieth centuries, and the partition of

Palestine by the UN in 1947 as sources of resentment and confrontation between the

West and the Islamic world. Further, the AOC group states that, "The Israeli-Palestinian

issue has become a key symbol of the rift between Western and Muslim societies and

remains one of the gravest threats to international stability" (2006, Highlights, p.1).

Similarly, the Crisis Group states that the festering Israeli-Palestinian conflict

significantly strengthens "the appeal of the most virulent and dangerous jihadi

tendencies" (2005, Executive Summary, p.1). For its part, the UN General Assembly

resolution cites "prolonged unresolved conflicts" as a "condition conducive to the spread

of terrorism" (2006, 4)--which certainly applies to the Israeli-Palestinian conflict as well

as to other conflicts such as in Kashmir and Chechnya.

The AOC group identifies globalization as a source of Islamic extremism and the

UN's resolution describes how socioeconomic marginalization associated with

globalization helps to spread Islamic extremism. The AOC report states that, "Aspects of

globalization have been experienced by many communities as an assault. For them, the

prospect of great well being has come at a high price, which included cultural

homogenization, family dislocation, challenges to traditional lifestyles, and environmental degradation" (2006, Highlights, p.1). Further, the report describes the world's economic divide by stating, "Our world is alarmingly out of balance. For many, the last century brought unprecedented progress, prosperity, and freedom. For others, it is marked an era of subjugation, humiliation and dispossession . . . a world where the income of the planet's three richest people is greater than the combined income of the world's least developed countries" (2006, Part I, p.1). Lastly, the report conveys how the West is driving globalization and at the same time is threatened by it, not only by Islamic extremism, but also by population flows from poor to rich countries and by unintegrated immigrant communities among other factors. The movements of people from the Middle East, North Africa and Southeast Asia to Europe are examples of this trend.

All three international organizations identify "apostate" or authoritarian Muslim governments as a source of Islamic extremism. The AOC report describes how Muslim governments are resistant to reform and suppress nonviolent political movements--key factors in the rise of extremism. Together these conditions "deprive many Muslim countries of the impetus, hope, and energy needed to achieve economic and social progress" (2006, Highlights, p.2). In the same vein, the UN resolution cites political exclusion and a lack of good governance as conditions that help to spread terrorism. The Crisis Group report describes how "internal" or nationalist Islamic extremists believe in the legitimacy of jihad against nominally Muslim regimes which they hold to be "impious" or apostate and thus targets for subversion.

The AOC group and Crisis Group reports identify non-Muslim rule or western military presence in Islamic lands as a source of Islamic extremism. The AOC's report states that, "Western military operations in Muslim countries contribute to a growing

56

climate of fear and animosity that is spreading around the world. The spiraling death toll in Iraq and the ongoing conflict in Afghanistan help swell the ranks of terrorist groups" (2006, Highlights, p.1). Looking at areas beyond Iraq, the Crisis Group report describes irredentists as Islamic extremists engaged in jihad to redeem land from non-Muslim rule or occupation in places such as Afghanistan, Chechnya, Kashmir, Mindanao in the southern Philippines, and Palestine.

Lastly, the Crisis Group contends that US policies in the Middle East and the way in which the GWOT is being conducted are sources of Islamic extremism from the standpoint that they exacerbate the existing problem of Islamic extremism. The report cites several US policies that it argues have aggravated the problem including: the failure to address the Israeli-Palestinian issue, the decision to make war on Iraq and the mishandling of the postwar situation, the resort to torture, the blanket stigmatization of all forms of jihad as terrorism, and the suspension of Western legal norms in respect to people accused of involvement in terrorism. While the AOC group does not specifically mention the US, the group's report does cite the perception of double standards in the application of international law and the protection of human rights as policies which increase resentment and the sense of vulnerability felt by many Muslims around the globe--a likely reference to US policy to use Guantanamo as a detention facility for terrorist suspects.

Of note, the AOC group contends that the root cause of the conflict between Islam and the West is political vice religious in nature. However, this conclusion is belied by the conclusion reached by all other groups in the study who found that religiously motivated extremist ideology is a principal source of Islamic extremism. Additionally, the AOC group's report seems to contradict itself by saying on the one hand that the issue is not religious in nature, but on the other hand identifying the debate on Islamic law and the interpretations of Islamic teachings as sources of friction in the Muslim world. This issue is developed further in Chapter 5, "Conclusions and Recommendations."

Secondary Research Question #3 (Nongovernmental organizations and civilian experts)

The third secondary research question is, What do NGOs and civilian experts identify as the sources of Islamic extremism? NGOs and civilian experts used for this research include two think tanks--the RAND Corporation (RAND) and the Center for Strategic and International Studies (CSIS)--and two academics--Bernard Lewis and John Esposito. The nongovernmental group identified seven principal sources of Islamic extremism: historical grievances, ideology, globalization, "apostate" or authoritarian Muslim governments, non-Muslim rule or western military presence in Islamic lands, external funding of Islamic fundamentalism and extremism, and US policies.

The group unanimously identified historical grievances as a source of Islamic extremism. RAND describes the Israeli-Palestinian conflict as one that has plagued the Middle East for more than a half a century and states, "Successive Arab defeats in armed conflicts with the Israelis have contributed to the discredit of Arab regimes and to the rise of Islamic extremism in the Arab world" (2004, 49). RAND contends that Kashmir serves the same function for extremists in Pakistan. CSIS writes that radical Islamist violence has numerous historical roots such as the reaction to colonialism in the early twentieth century (2004, 4). Lewis argues that "much of the anger in the Islamic world is directed against the Westerner, seen as the ancient and immemorial enemy of Islam since the first clashes between the Muslim caliphs and the Christian emperors" (2004, 132).

Lastly, Esposito describes how Islamic extremists justify violence by reciting a litany of Muslim grievances such as the Crusades, European colonialism, the creation of Israel, and the Cold War (2003, 73).

NGOs and civilian experts also unanimously identify radical ideology as a source of Islamic extremism. RAND describes how extremist ideologues like Usama bin Laden, without any religious training or authority, hijack religious symbols and rhetoric for their own extremist interpretation of Islam--a problem it says is exacerbated by the decentralization of religious authority in Sunni Islam (2004, 39). CSIS states that the ideological nature of the threat is one of its most dangerous aspects (2004, 5). Lewis conveys that the extremists' ideology involves "a return to true Islam, including the abolition of all the laws and other social borrowings from the West and the restoration of the Islamic Holy Law, the shari'a, as the effective law of the land" (2004, 134). Regarding the extremists' ideology, Espisoto states that, "Some Muslims, a radicalized minority, combine militancy with messianic visions to inspire and mobilize an army of God whose jihad they believe will liberate Muslims at home and abroad" (2003, 27).

RAND, Lewis and Esposito identify globalization as a source of Islamic extremism. RAND describes how anger in the Muslim world is directed against the US because, "as the chief agent of global change, the United States represents the forces that, in the view of some Muslims, have placed their countries in a position of inferiority vis-à-vis the West and threaten the integrity of Muslim societies and values" (2004, 39). Further, RAND argues that the emergence of mass media under the auspices of globalization exacerbates extremism with the advent of satellite outlets like al-Jazeera who reinforce narratives of Arab victimization (2004, 46). Lewis contends that many

59

Muslims view globalization as American economic penetration. Further, he argues that almost the entire Muslim world is affected by poverty and tyranny and that both of these problems are attributed by Muslims to America (2004, 113). Esposito sees globalization in the next century as one factor that will strain relations between Islam and the West. "The twenty-first century will be dominated by the global encounter of two major and rapidly growing world religions, Christianity and Islam, and by the forces of globalization that will strain relations between the West and the rest" (2003, xii).

RAND, Lewis, and Esposito also identify "apostate" or authoritarian Muslim governments as a source of Islamic extremism. RAND describes how the failure of postindependence models and states has led to extremism. "The residue of the failed political experiments of the postcolonial era is a set of repressive, corrupt, and unrepresentative regimes incapable of providing a modicum of democracy, economic well-being, or social justice" (2004, 37). Lewis conveys the extremists' view that apostate governments must be removed. "The Islamic world, in their [extremist] view, has taken a wrong turning. Its rulers call themselves Muslims and make a pretense of Islam, but they are in fact apostates who have *abrogated* [abolish or annul] the Holy Law and adopted foreign and infidel laws and customs. The only solution, for them, is a return to the authentic Muslim way of life, and for this removal of the apostate governments is an essential first step" (2004, 24). Similarly, Esposito argues that extremists believe jihad is required against authoritarian governments. "Many Muslims today believe that the conditions of their world require a jihad. They look around them and see a world dominated by corrupt authoritarian governments" (2003, 27).

Non-Muslim rule or western military presence in Islamic lands is identified by RAND, Lewis and Esposito as a source of Islamic extremism. RAND describes how millions of Muslims from all over the world went to Afghanistan to fight against non-Muslim Soviet occupation; many subsequently played a key role in other campaigns of extremist violence in Algeria, Egypt, Bosnia, Chechnya, Kashmir and Southeast Asia (2004, 47-48). Further, RAND describes how the war in Iraq is the first time since the withdrawal of European colonial powers that a Western country has assumed governance of a Muslim country (2004, 52). Lewis emphasizes the importance of territorial issues to Islamic extremists citing Israel as an example: "No peace or compromise with Israel is possible, any concession is only a step toward the true final solution--the dissolution of the State of Israel, the return of the land to its true owner, the Muslim Palestinians" (2004, 150). Esposito describes similar struggles over territory perceived as Islamic lands, such as in Kashmir, Chechnya, Dagestan, the southern Philippines, Bosnia, and Kosovo (2003, 26).

The nongovernmental group is unanimous in identifying external funding of Islamic fundamentalism and extremism as a source of Islamic extremism. RAND states that, "Saudi funding and export of the Wahhabi version of Islam over the past three decades has had the effect, whether intended or not, of promoting the growth of religious extremism throughout the Muslim world" (2004, 41). Financed in part by external funding, CSIS describes how, "In Pakistan, the madrassas, mosques, and jihadi sectarian groups form a dangerous triangle of terrorist breeding grounds and reinforce each other's messages of anti-Westernism and anti-secularism" (2004, 12). In addition to funding extremist teachings in the Muslim world, Lewis argues that external funding also finds its way into Western countries. "Even in Western countries in Europe and America, where the public education systems are good, Wahhabi indoctrination centers may be the only form of Islamic education available to new converts and to Muslim parents who wish to give their children some grounding in their own inherited religious and cultural tradition. This indoctrination is provided in private schools, religious seminars, mosque schools, holiday camps, and increasingly, prisons" (2004, 128). Lastly, Esposito describes how "Saudi Arabia created state-financed international Islamic organizations to promote its Wahhabi-based, pan-Islamic vision and ideology. Established in 1962, the World Islamic League vigorously engaged in an energetic international dawah, preaching and propagating Wahhabi Islam to other Muslims (as well as non-Muslims), financing the building of mosques, schools, libraries, hospitals, and clinics" (2003, 107).

Lastly, the nongovernmental group unanimously identified US policies as a source of Islamic extremism. According to the RAND report, US policies that cause anti-US and anti-Western sentiment include the US military presence in Saudi Arabia, Afghanistan and Iraq. The CSIS report describes how US policy plays into the calculus and states that, "two exacerbating conditions--the lack of a Middle East Peace Process and the war in Iraq--have strengthened the appeal of the ideology" (2004, 6). Lewis argues that US policy to support authoritarian and corrupt Muslim governments is increasingly a grievance among Islamic extremists" (2004, 102). In the strongest criticism of US polices, Esposito contends that US policies such as its "unilateral approach" to the war in Iraq, and one-sided rhetoric toward the Israeli-Palestinian conflict, Chechnya and Kashmir have fueled widespread anger and anti-Americanism in the Muslim world.

Secondary Research Question #4 (Islamic extremists)

The final secondary research question is, What do Islamic extremists identify as the sources of their grievances? The research considered the views of Taqi ad-Din Ahmed ibn Taymiyya, Hassan al-Banna, Sayyid Qutb and Usama bin Laden. Extremists identified five principal sources of Islamic extremism: historical grievances, globalization, "apostate" or authoritarian Muslim governments, non-Muslim rule or western military presence in Islamic lands, and US policies.

Usama bin Laden's comments about the Crusades being an attack on Islam, European Imperialism and the theft of Palestine reflect what he views as historical grievances. Additionally, in a 2001 letter read on al-Jazeera, bin Laden argued that the US attack on Afghanistan was a Crusade against Islam and that it is part of the ongoing onslaught by the West against Muslims dating back to the end of World War I. In the letter Bin Laden states, "Since World War One, which ended over 83 years ago, the entire Islamic world has fallen under the Crusader banners, under the British, French and Italian governments" (2001).

Al-Banna, Qutb and bin Laden all identify globalization or Westernization as a grievance. Al-Banna considered Europe and the West as a physical and intellectual threat to Islam. Concerned about Western-style education, Al-Banna called for an end to Westernization and what he called the "mental colonization" of Muslims (Habeck 2006, 30). Like al-Banna, Qutb wrote before the advent of today's system of globalization. Still, his anti-Western and anti-American beliefs were evident by his criticism of capitalism and personal freedoms. Qutb writes, "Look at this capitalism with its monopolies, its *usury* [charging of interest] . . . at this individual freedom . . . at this

63

materialistic attitude which deadens the spirit . . . at this behavior, like animals, which you call 'mixing of the sexes'; at this vulgarity which you call emancipation of women" (Esposito 2002, 57). Lastly, in his 2002 letter *To the Americans* bin Laden argues that his grievances against the US-led globalization system include the pervasiveness of corrupt societal and economic systems penetrating the Muslim world. "You steal our wealth and oil at paltry prices because of your international influence and military threats. . . . You are a nation that permits acts of immorality, and you consider these acts to be pillars of personal freedom. . . . You are nation that permits usury, which has been forbidden by all religions."

All four of the extremist ideologues considered for this research identified "apostate" or authoritarian Muslim governments as a source of their grievances. Writing in the thirteenth century, Taymiyya argued that the Muslim Mongol rulers were apostates because they did not strictly adhere to sharia law and therefore, jihad against them was required. In his book *Milestones*, Qutb also argued that Muslim governments were not using sharia law and were therefore *jahiliyya* (ignorant or exhibiting un-Islamic behavior). Qutb writes of apostate Muslims, "all the existing so-called 'Muslim' societies are also jahili societies. . . . Although they believe in the Unity of God, still they have relegated the legislative attribute of God to others and submit to this authority, and from this authority they derive their systems, their traditions and customs, their laws, their values and standards, and almost every practice of life" (Qutb 1964, 82-83). In a 2004 letter posted on the website of the *Global Islamic Media Front,* bin Laden claimed that the Saudi government had betrayed its people, become a client of America and should be deposed by force. "The Saudi regime has committed very serious acts of disobedience. . .

. Millions of people suffer every day from poverty and depravation, while millions of riyals flow into the bank accounts of the royals. . . . It has got to the point where the regime has gone so far as to be clearly beyond the pale of Islam, allying itself with infidel America and aiding it against Muslims" (2004).

Bin Laden also identifies non-Muslim rule or western military presence in Islamic lands and US policies in general as grievances. In a letter to Saudi scholars, bin Laden described the stationing of US troops in Saudi Arabia as a violation of the umma. "The enemy has invaded the land of our umma, violated her honor, shed her blood, and occupied her sanctuaries. This aggression has reached such a catastrophic and disastrous point as to have brought about a calamity unprecedented in the history of our umma, namely the invasion by the American and western Crusader forces of the Arabian Peninsula and Saudi Arabia" (circa 1995). Regarding US policies, again in his 2002 letter *To the Americans,* bin Laden describes what he holds to be the offensive US policies across the Muslim world in Palestine, Somalia, Chechnya, Kashmir, Lebanon, Iraq, Afghanistan, and in supporting "apostate" Muslim governments.

<u>Primary Research Question</u>

The primary research question this thesis seeks to answer is: Has the *NSS* properly identified the sources of Islamic extremism? The analysis suggests that significant differences exist among the various groups as to the sources of Islamic extremism--not all of which are accounted for in the *NSS*.

Whereas the *NSS* identifies the sources of Islamic extremism as: (1) terrorism that springs from political alienation, (2) grievances that can be blamed on others, (3) subcultures of conspiracy and misinformation, (4) an ideology that justifies murder, (5) not the inevitable by-product of poverty, (6) not simply a result of hostility to US policy in Iraq, (7) not simply a response to our efforts to prevent terror attacks, and (8) not simply a result of Israeli-Palestinian issues; the analysis of the perspectives considered in answering the secondary research questions suggests that the sources of Islamic extremism are: (1) historical grievances, (2) extremist ideology, (3) globalization, (4) "apostate" or authoritarian Muslim governments, (5) non-Muslim rule or western military presence in Islamic lands, (6) external funding of Islamic fundamentalism and extremism, and (7) US policies.

Of note, a cross-reference of what the different perspectives identify as the sources of Islamic extremism is graphically depicted in Appendix A, "Data Display Matrix."

## Summary and Conclusions

This chapter analyzed the sources of Islamic extremism in order to answer the primary and secondary research questions. The answers to the four secondary research questions provided the foundation of data necessary to answer the primary research question. Based on the research and answers to the secondary questions, the analysis suggests that the *NSS* does not properly identify the sources of Islamic extremism. Chapter 5 will expand on this conclusion as well as make several recommendations for action and for further study.

# CHAPTER 5

## CONCLUSIONS AND RECOMMENDATIONS

> The United States is a nation engaged in what will be a long war. Since the attacks of September 11, 2001, our nation has fought a global war against violent extremists who use terrorism as their weapon of choice, and who seek to destroy our free way of life. Currently, the struggle is centered in Iraq and Afghanistan, but we will need to be prepared and arranged to successfully defend our Nation and its interests around the globe for years to come. (2006, v)
>
> *Quadrennial Defense Report Review*

## Introduction

The purpose of this thesis is to: conduct a qualitative analysis of the sources of Islamic extremism from multiple perspectives, determine if the *NSS* properly identifies the sources of Islamic extremism, and make recommendations on how to counter the sources of Islamic extremism and improve US security and counterterrorism strategy.

This chapter draws conclusions about the sources of Islamic extremism and makes recommendations on how to improve US security and counterterrorism strategy. Additionally, this chapter identifies areas that are beyond the scope of this thesis but merit further study.

This chapter is organized into four parts: introduction, conclusions and recommendations, areas for further study, and conclusion.

## Conclusions and Recommendations

Listed below are 12 conclusions reached during the thesis research and analysis. Where appropriate, recommendations immediately follow their associated conclusions.

1. Sources of Islamic Extremism. The analysis in Chapter 4 suggests that the *NSS* does not properly identify the sources of Islamic extremism. Rather, this thesis concludes that the sources of Islamic extremism are: historical grievances, extremist ideology, globalization, "apostate" or authoritarian Muslim governments, non-Muslim rule or western military presence in Islamic lands, external funding of Islamic fundamentalism and extremism, and US policies.

However, there are multiple points of agreement between the sources of Islamic extremism identified in the *NSS* and the sources as concluded by this thesis. Areas of agreement include the following sources of Islamic extremism (*NSS* / thesis): political alienation / "apostate" or authoritarian Muslim governments, grievances that can be blamed on others / historical grievances, an ideology that justifies murder / extremist ideology, and our efforts to prevent terror attacks / US policies.

Principal points of disagreement include: the *NSS* seems to inappropriately de-emphasize the importance of the Iraq War and the Israeli-Palestinian issue as sources of Islamic extremism, the *NSS* does not identify non-Muslim rule or western military presence in Islamic land as a source of extremism beyond its' mention of Iraq and Israel, and the *NSS* does not identify globalization or the external funding of Islamic fundamentalism and extremism as sources of Islamic extremism.

Recommendations: (1) Revise what the *NSS* identifies as the sources of Islamic extremism; doing so establishes a better framework under which all elements of national power implement policy relating to countering Islamic extremism; (2) at a minimum, while the *NSS* currently proposes strategies to mitigate the four principal areas that it contends give rise to terrorism, the *NSS* should offer counter strategies for all eight areas that it identifies as giving rise to terrorism.

2. Not Any One Source. The *NSS* argues that terrorism is not simply the result of poverty, not simply a result of hostility to US policy in Iraq, not simply a result of Israeli-Palestinian issues, and not simply a response to US efforts to prevent terror attacks. This thesis concludes that Islamic extremism is not simply the result of any one factor or source. Rather, what is a source of Islamic extremism for one person may not be for another; what is a source in one country may not be in another. Taken together, the sources constitute the body of issues that give rise to Islamic extremism across the Muslim world.

3. Some Sources Are Immitigable. Conventional wisdom suggests that if you can identify the source of a problem, then you can address the source and solve the problem. However, the research suggests that while some sources of Islamic extremism such as authoritarian Muslim governments and external funding of extremism can and should be addressed, other sources such as nineteenth century European imperialism and the Crusades cannot be mitigated.

4. Islamic Extremists Are A Minority. The NIE states that Islamic extremists, although a small percentage of Muslims, are increasing in both number and geographic dispersion. Most Muslims are not extremists and it cannot be overstated that Islamic extremists are a minority in the Muslim world. Further, many argue that the principle fight against Islamic extremists should occur in the Muslim world between the minority extremists and the majority moderates.

Recommendations: (1) Take a more discriminatory approach toward Islamism, the different types of extremist groups (e.g., nationalist, irredentist and transnational), and the concept of jihad; (2) understand that some forms of Islamism such as political Islamism are positive as is jihad when referring to a Muslim's internal struggle to resist temptation and evil; (3) continue to support moderate Muslims in their fight against extremism in the form of financial aid, intelligence sharing, and training and equipment for security services.

5. Importance of the Israeli-Palestinian Issue. The *NSS* states that terrorism is not simply a result of Israeli-Palestinian issues. While true from the standpoint that no one issue is singularly responsible for the threat of Islamic terrorism, it is also true that no other issue is more commonly cited as a source of friction between the Muslim world and the West; a situation that is frequently exploited by Islamic extremists.

Recommendations: (1) Reinvigorate the Middle East peace process in conjunction with countries in the region and the international community in order to establish two sovereign states and address grievances of both parties; (2) success is dependent upon the US and moderate Arab governments pressuring both sides to make concessions necessary to reach a settlement.

6. The Iraq War and Islamic Extremism. The *NSS* states that terrorism is not simply a result of hostility to US policy in Iraq, which appears to de-emphasize the importance of the Iraq war to the cause of Islamic extremists. Again, the assertion is true from the standpoint that no one issue is *the* source of Islamic extremism. However, the research suggests that the Iraq war is of greater relative importance to the Islamic extremist movement than that attributed to it in the *NSS*. The NIE captures the essence of

70

the body of research related to the Iraq war when it states, "The Iraq conflict has become the 'cause celebre' for jihadists, breeding a deep resentment of US involvement in the Muslim world and cultivating supporters for the global jihadist movement" (2006, 2).

Of note, in spite of the conclusion that the US war in Iraq is a source of Islamic extremism spawning such offshoots as al-Qaida in Iraq, anecdotal evidence suggests that the vast majority of Muslims killed in Iraq are killed by other Muslims--a trend appropriately attributable to interfaith rivalry and extremism.

Recommendations: (1) Acknowledge in the *NSS* the criticality of the Iraq war as a source of Islamic extremism; (2) understand that while a US presence in Iraq is a boon for extremist recruiting, extremist success in Iraq would inspire them to fight elsewhere much like the mujahedeen from the Afghan-Soviet War were inspired to fight elsewhere after the withdrawal of the Soviets; (3) continue supporting the Iraqi government to be an example of political inclusion vice repression to other Muslim governments in the Middle East; (4) as soon as is practical, realign needed resources from Iraq to other areas involved in the broader fight against Islamic extremism (e.g., Afghanistan, North Africa, etc.).

7. External Funding of Islamic Extremism and Radical Education. *The 9/11 Commission Report,* RAND, CSIS, Lewis and Esposito all identify the external funding of Islamic extremism and radical education as sources of Islamic extremism. These groups and individuals specifically mention Saudi Arabia among Persian Gulf countries as a source of funding for Islamic extremism and Pakistan owing to the radical education in its madrassas.

Recommendations to curb external funding: (1) work with the governments of countries at both ends of the funding stream--the source and destination--to deny resources to extremists; (2) conduct a critical review of intermediaries--banks and radical Islamic NGOs--who facilitate the flow of funds to extremists; (3) support moderate Muslim NGOs and international NGOs to provide an alternative for individuals in need of social services.

Recommendations to moderate radical education: (1) Provide financial assistance to moderate curriculum and leader training and education, (2) work bilaterally and with international bodies to review educational materials, and (3) increase the number of educational exchange programs with Muslim countries.

8. Internet Sanctuary. Historically, insurgent or guerilla forces have utilized physical sanctuaries for activities such as training, equipping and operational planning. Two obvious examples are Cambodia for the Viet Cong and Pakistan for the Taliban and al-Qaida forces.

In the current conflict, some activities previously done almost exclusively from a physical sanctuary are now being done via a virtual sanctuary on the Internet. The State Department's annual terrorism report describes how al-Qaida has transitioned from a structured network to a diffuse network of like-minded individuals since the loss of their sanctuary base in Afghanistan after 11 September 2001. As a result, some individuals in this new generation of extremists have become, "radicalized 'virtually,' meeting in cyberspace and gaining their training and expertise in part from what they glean from the Internet" (2006, Ch. 2, p. 2). Further, the NIE judges radicalization is growing more quickly and anonymously in the Internet age (2006, 3-4).

72

Recommendations: (1) Acknowledge in US policy documents the use and importance of the Internet to extremists' recruiting, training, fund-raising, indoctrination and information operations efforts; (2) implement oversight necessary to ensure there exists a sufficient and appropriate mix of US government resources to counter extremists' use of the Internet as a facilitation tool for their operations; (3) ensure sufficient interagency intelligence personnel and expertise are leveraged in order to exploit points of intelligence value from extremists' use of the Internet; and (4) seek to enact laws (national and international) which preclude the use of the Internet to incite or facilitate terrorism.

9. Extremist Ideology and Moderate Muslims. Habeck's comments about the extremists' use of the Quran to justify their actions are representative of the body of research for this thesis. Habeck states that, "The discussion of Quran'ic verses and hadith on jihad, more than on any other topic, shows the willingness of the jihadis to pick and choose which texts they will and will not accept as valid for Muslims today. The emphasis is always on those parts of the books that define jihad as fighting and that paint the relationship between believer and unbeliever in the bleakest terms. Jihadis never mention the texts that talk about tolerance or peace and have declared invalid an important hadith that calls the internal struggle to follow God the "greater jihad" and fighting the "lesser jihad" (2006, 53).

Recommendations: (1) Acknowledge that the fight over the interpretation of holy text is primarily one within the Muslim world between moderates and extremists; (2) support Muslim governments and moderate Muslim scholars and religious leaders whose interpretations of the holy texts enable peaceful coexistence with modernity.

10. Guantanamo: Asset or Liability? Several perspectives considered in this study have criticized US policy to use Guantanamo detention facilities to hold terror suspects--a policy which fosters anti-American sentiment, undermines U.S. credibility, and is unpopular with moderate Muslims, US allies (particularly in Europe) and some Americans. For example, Esposito states that, "The detention of individuals for indefinite periods without trial or access to evidence, raise deep concerns about the erosion of civil liberties and human rights for Arabs and Muslims, and others as well" (2003, 152). The AOC group and the Crisis Group raise similar concerns about the suspension of legal norms regarding terrorism suspects as have moderate Muslims, US allies and American citizens. While a double standard seems to apply here vis-à-vis Islamic extremists' treatment of their captives (e.g., kidnapping victims), the costs to the US of operating the Guantanamo detention facilities seem to outweigh its benefits.

Recommendations: (1) Once information of intelligence value is obtained, try terror suspects either in the US, international court, the country where the offense occurred, or in their country of residence; and (2) review laws and conventions (national and international) to ensure adequate fidelity exists to detain, categorize and try terror suspects.

11. Multinational and Inter-Agency Cooperation. The research suggests a difference in what the US, Europeans, international organizations, and US allies identify as the sources of Islamic extremism and how best to approach defeating terrorism.

As was mentioned earlier, the UN-sponsored AOC group's report takes the position that, ". . . although religion if often cynically exploited to stir passions, fuel suspicions, and support alarmist claims that he world if facing a new 'war of religion',

74

the root of the matter is political" (Press Release, p.1). In a similar vein, the UN resolution's list of conditions conducive to the spread of terrorism omits any reference to the religious nature of the conflict. However, all other perspectives considered during this thesis research concluded that religiously motivated extremist ideology is a principal source of Islamic extremism. For example, the 9/11 Commission's stance is that for Islamic extremists, politics and religion are inseparable. The Commission's report states, "That stream [extremist stream of Islam] is motivated by religion and does not distinguish politics from religion, thus distorting both" (2004, 362).

The analysis, therefore, suggests there is a significant point of disagreement between the UN and AOC group on the one hand, and the US government, NGOs and civilian experts, and the other international organization considered (Crisis Group) on the other regarding the religious versus political nature of the conflict.

Additionally, within the agencies of the US government there seem to be points of disagreement in terms of identifying the sources of Islamic extremism and how best to counter them. For example, whereas the *NSS* focuses on ideology as a source of Islamic extremism and de-emphasizes the importance of the war in Iraq, the NIE focuses on the war in Iraq. Similarly, the State Department's annual report on terrorism and the NIE seems to place greater emphasis on extremists' use of the Internet than do other US government agencies.

Recommendations: (1) Intensify bilateral and multinational dialogue and cooperation (e.g., with the UN, NATO, Pakistan, Saudi Arabia, and others) to gain a common understanding of the sources of Islamic extremism and to improve measures to prevent and combat terrorism; (2) within the US government, reinvigorate processes

75

where dialogue and cooperation between different agencies results in a common understanding and approach to dealing with the sources of Islamic extremism.

12. Islamic Extremism and National Policy. This thesis judges that some US national policy decisions such as the decision to invade Iraq have had the unintended consequence of becoming sources of Islamic extremism in the Muslim world. This thesis does not argue that the potentiality of that effect should drive policy formulation. However, how US policy is perceived in the Muslim world should play into the cost-benefit-risk calculus of national policy formulation. Additionally, as concluded by *The 9/11 Commission Report*, long-term US policy success against Islamic extremism requires the balanced use of all elements of national power.

Recommendations: (1) Return to a *NSS* which describes US national interests in terms of being vital, important, or peripheral; this construct is helpful in setting parameters for policy makers to then determine what level of risk is appropriate commensurate with the national interest; (2) balance the use of military and nonmilitary elements of national power to address holistically the political, economic and ideological aspects of Islamic extremism.

## Further Study

This study recommends six topics for further study. All of them, in one way, shape or form, are critically important to the fight against Islamic extremism now and for the foreseeable future.

1. Extremism among Muslim Diasporas. How can the US and its allies address the growth of Islamic extremism among diasporas in Europe as evidenced by extremists' networks inside Europe as well as by the Madrid and London terrorist attacks?

2. Islamic Extremism in North Africa. How can the US and its allies address the growth of Islamic extremism in North Africa (e.g., Algeria, Morocco, Egypt, Somalia, etc.) particularly given the confluence of factors in that area including: colonial ties between Africa and Europe which facilitates travel between the continents, and ungoverned spaces in Africa which are conducive to extremist operations?

3. Globalization and Extremes of Rich and Poor. Much of the Muslim world views globalization as American economic penetration and is affected by poverty and tyranny. Further, moderate Muslims and extremists cite as a grievance the extremes of rich and poor between the US, the elites in Saudi Arabia, Kuwait, et al. and average Muslims. However, the contrast between rich and poor is a global issue, not just an issue of Islam versus the West. How to overcome this issue merits further study and is likely one whose solution lies beyond the efforts of any one country.

4. The Israeli-Palestinian Conflict. How can an equitable solution to the Israeli-Palestinian conflict be achieved which would result in the establishment of two sovereign states and address grievances of both parties (e.g., access to holy sites and right of return, etc.)?

5. US-Saudi Arabia Policy. How can the US improve its policy toward Saudi Arabia to better control external funding of Islamic fundamentalism and extremism?

6. US-Pakistan Policy. How can the US improve its policy toward Pakistan in order to address radical Islamic madrassa education and the rise of Islamic extremism particularly in the Federally Administered Tribal Area (FATA) where it has a direct impact on coalition operations in Afghanistan, as well as on global terrorism operations and planning?

## Conclusion

The 11 September 2001 attacks and many other terrorist attacks before them have demonstrated that Islamic extremism is a threat to the United States. Therefore, it is critically important that the US properly identify the sources of Islamic extremism and design a strategy that employs the balanced use of all elements of national power to defeat or mitigate this threat. The aim of this thesis was to research and identify the sources of Islamic extremism and determine if the current *NSS* properly identifies the sources of Islamic extremism. However, the extremist enemy will adapt, circumstances will change, and some sources of Islamic extremism may change. Therefore, it will require a concerted and continuous effort on the part of the US government and others to maintain currency on the sources of Islamic extremism and adjust US policy accordingly in order to defeat this threat.

## Analysis of the Sources of Islamic Extremism

| Nat'l Security Strategy | Other U.S. Gov't | Int'l Organizations | NGOs & Experts | Islamic Extremists | Conclusion |
|---|---|---|---|---|---|
| • Political alienation<br>• Grievances that can be blamed on others<br>• Sub-cultures of conspiracy and misinformation<br>• An ideology that justifies murder<br><br>• Not the inevitable by-product of poverty<br>• Not simply a result to U.S. policy in Iraq<br>• Not simply a response to our efforts to prevent terror attacks<br>• Not simply a result of Israeli-Palestinian issues | **NSCT:**<br>• NSS points plus others<br>• Western influence in Muslim world<br>• Apostate governments<br>• Re-establish caliphate<br><br>**9/11 Commission Report:**<br>• Ideology<br>• Political & economic malaise in Middle East<br>• Iranian Revolution<br>• U.S. aggression against Muslims<br>• U.S. support to repressive rulers<br>• U.S. troops in Saudi Arabia<br>• U.S. Middle East policies<br>• Suffering of Iraqi people due to U.S. sanctions<br>• U.S. support to Israel<br>• Modernization & Globalization<br>• Conflicts in the world involving Muslims<br>• Afghan-Soviet War<br>• Saudi oil wealth & Wahhabi promotion<br>• Confluence of Afghan refugees, strained Pakistani education system & Wahhabism<br><br>**National Intel Estimate:**<br>• Entrenched grievances such as corruption, injustice & fear of Western domination<br>• The Iraq "jihad"<br>• Slow pace of economic, social & political reforms<br>• Pervasive anti-U.S. sentiment among most Muslims<br><br>**DoS Terrorism Country Rep.:**<br>• Ideology & propaganda<br>• The Iraq War<br>• The internet<br><br>**NMSP-WOT:**<br>• Ideology<br>• Anti-Westernization<br>• Re-establish caliphate | **UN General Assembly:**<br>• Prolonged unresolved conflicts<br>• Lack of rule of law & violations of human rights<br>• Lack of good governance<br>• Political exclusion<br>• Socio-economic marginalization<br>• Dehumanization of victims of terrorism<br>• Ethnic, national and religious discrimination<br><br>**UN Alliance of Civilizations:**<br>• Globalization<br>• Western policies affecting Muslim countries<br>  – Western military operations in Muslim countries<br>  – Perception of double standard in int'l law application<br>  – Israeli-Palestinian conflict<br>• Trends in Muslim societies<br>  – Debate between progressive & regressive forces<br>  – Interpretations of Islamic teachings<br>  – Resistance to reform & political repression<br><br>**International Crisis Group:**<br>• Non-Muslim rule in Islamic land<br>• Iraq War<br>• Afghan-Soviet War<br>• Apostate Muslim gov'ts<br>• Extremist ideology<br>• Israeli-Palestinian conflict<br>• Way in which the GWOT is being waged:<br>  – Resort to torture<br>  – Blanket stigmatization of all forms of jihad as terrorism<br>  – Suspense of legal norms (e.g., GTMO) | **RAND Corporation**<br>• Failed pol. & econ. models<br>• Iranian Revolution<br>• Structural anti-Westernism<br>• Emergence of mass media<br>• Decentralization of religious authority<br>• Islamic resurgence<br>• Arabization of non-Arab Muslims vs. local tradition<br>• Convergence of Islamism & tribalism<br>• Ext. funding of extremism (Saudi Wahhabi funding)<br>• Radical Islamic networks<br>• IS-PA & Kashmir conflicts<br>• Afghan-Soviet War<br>• Gulf War of 1991<br>• Iraq War<br>• 9/11 & GWOT<br><br>**CSIS:**<br>• Extremist ideology<br>• U.S. Middle East policies<br>  – Iraq War<br>  – Lack of a Middle East peace process<br>• Four contributing factors:<br>  – Poverty<br>  – Demographics<br>  – Muslim NGOs<br>  – Radicalization of educ. (madrassas)<br><br>**Bernard Lewis:**<br>• Apostate Muslim gov'ts<br>• Extremist ideology<br>• Globalization<br>  – Westernization<br>  – Poverty; disparity<br>• "Marriage of Saudi power and Wahhabi teaching"<br>• Establishment of Israel & Western support to Israel<br>• Imperialism<br>• Defeat of Soviets in 1989<br>• Gulf War 1991 & sanctions<br><br>**John Esposito**<br>• Historical grievances (Crusades, colonialism etc)<br>• Corrupt authoritarian gov't<br>• Afghan-Soviet War<br>• U.S. policies (Israel, Iraq)<br>• Westernization<br>• Wahhabism & maddrassas<br>• Extremist ideas / ideology | **Taqi ad-Din ibn Taymiyya:**<br>• Apostate Muslim gov'ts<br>  – e.g., Muslim Mongols<br>• Anti-secularism<br>  – Only pure sharia law<br><br>**Hassan Al-Banna:**<br>• Extremist ideology<br>  – Only sharia acceptable<br>  – Anti-secularism<br>  – Anti-Westernization<br>• Apostate Muslim gov'ts<br>• Historical grievances<br>  – Colonialism<br>  – Imperialism<br><br>**Sayyid Qutb:**<br>• Extremist ideology<br>  – Only sharia acceptable<br>  – Anti-secularism<br>  – Anti-Westernization<br>  – Ultra-conservative<br>  – Offensive jihad<br>  – Literal interpretation<br>• Islam vs jayiliyya-ignorance<br>  – Apostates are jayiliyya<br>  – West is jayiliyya<br>  – Entire world in state of jayiliyya<br>• Apostate Muslim gov'ts<br><br>**Usama bin Laden**<br>• Extremist Ideology<br>  – Anti-Westernization<br>  – Only sharia acceptable<br>  – Offensive jihad<br>  – Ultra-traditional; anti-modernity<br>  – Literal interpretation<br>• Historical grievances<br>  – Crusades<br>  – Caliphate<br>  – European colonialism<br>  – Est. of state of Israel<br>• West attacks against Islam<br>  – Israel-Palestin. conflict<br>  – Kashmir, Somalia, Chechnya, Lebanon, etc.<br>  – Afghan-Soviet War<br>  – U.S. support to Israel<br>  – U.S. troops S. Arabia<br>  – 1991 Iraq War & sanctions<br>• Apostate Muslim gov'ts<br>• Western imperialism (oil) | **Historical grievances:**<br>• Crusades<br>• Caliphate<br>• Establishment of Israel<br>• Imperialism / colonialism<br><br>**Extremist ideology:**<br>• Ultraconservative worldview; anti-modernity<br>• Literal text interpretation<br>• Sharia vs. secularism<br>• Offensive & defensive jihad<br>  – Islam vs. jayiliyya<br><br>**Globalization (econ & pol):**<br>• Westernization (culture)<br>  – Americanization<br>• Modernization<br>• Poverty; econ. disparity<br>• Secularism vs. sharia<br>• Emergence of mass media<br><br>**Apostate/Auth. Muslim gov't:**<br>• Use elements of secularism<br>• Failed pol. & econ. models<br>• Supported by West. gov'ts<br>• Failure to achieve progress on Israeli-Palestinian issue<br>• Corruption; lack of good governance<br><br>**Non-Muslim rule / military presence in Islamic land**<br>• Israeli-Palestinian conflict<br>• Afghan-Soviet War<br>• Iraq War 1991 & sanctions<br>• U.S. troops in Saudi Arabia<br>• Kashmir, Chechnya, Philippines, etc.<br>• Iraq War (OIF)<br>• Afghanistan War (OEF)<br><br>**External funding of Islamic fundamentalism / extremism**<br>• Saudi funding of Wahhabi<br>  – Fueled by petrodollars<br>• Radical madrassas (Pak)<br>• Growth of radical Islamic networks<br><br>**U.S. policies:**<br>• U.S. support to Israel<br>• Lack of M.E. peace process<br>• Gulf War / sanctions & OIF<br>• Susp. of legal norms-GTMO<br>• Resort to torture |

79

# APPENDIX B: MAPS

## Middle East

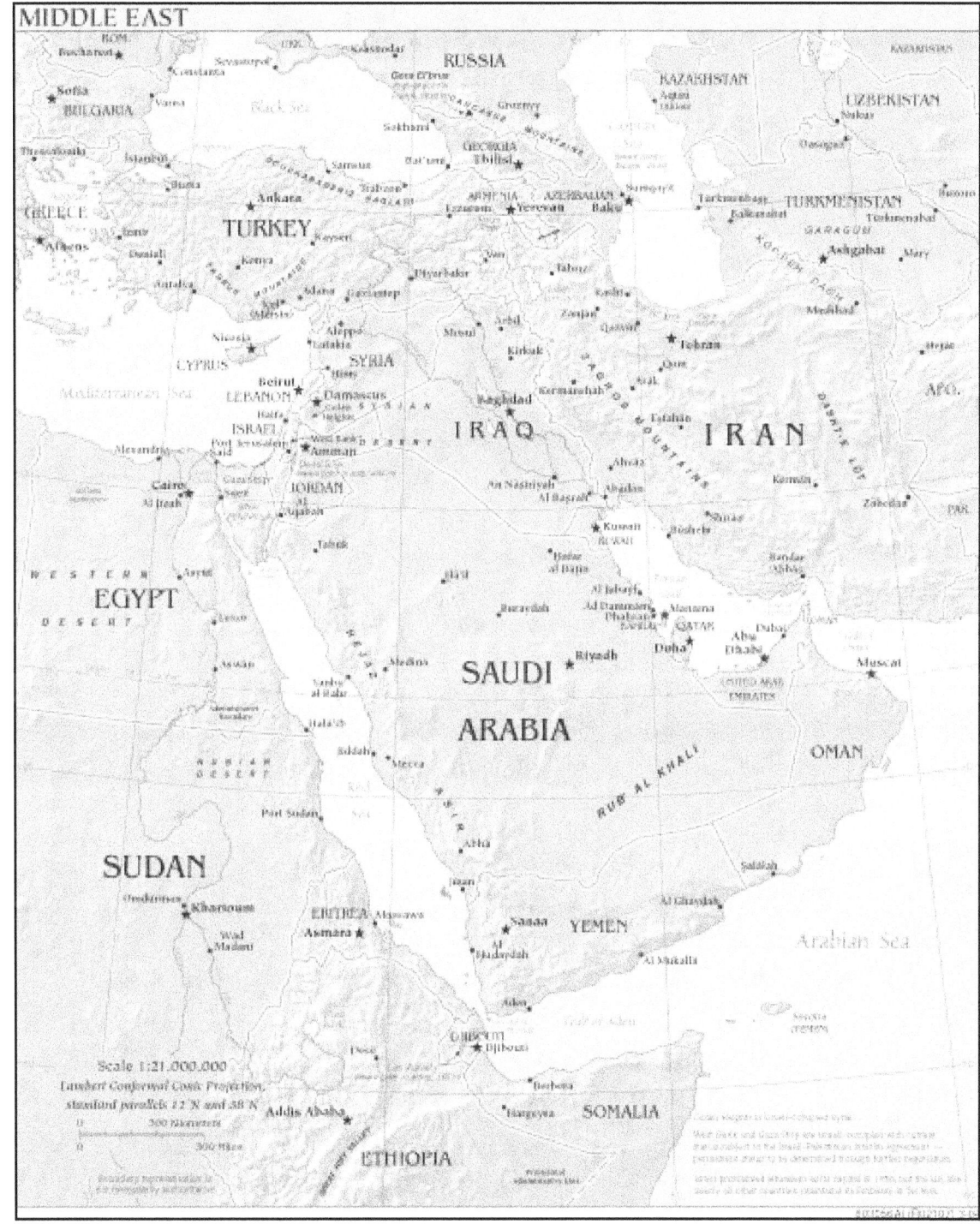

(Central Intelligence Agency 2006)

# Islamic Caliphate

# Ottoman Empire

# GLOSSARY

Abrogate. Abolish, annul, repeal or revoke.

Apostate. One who has abandoned their religious faith, principles or cause.

Caliph. Ruler of Islamic state.

Caliphate. Pan-Islamic state.

Colonialism. Policy whereby a nation maintains control over foreign dependencies.

Contributing factor. Something that helps to cause.

Dar al-Harb. Non-Islamic territory.

Dar al-Islam. Area of the world historically subject to Muslim rule.

Diaspora. Dispersion of people from their original homeland.

Facism. Political theory advocating authoritarian hierarchical government (as opposed to democracy or liberalism); established by Mussolini in Italy 1922-43.

Fatwa. Religious ruling or edict.

Fundamentalism. Rigid adherence to literal interpretation of a holy text; oppose excessive modernization as a betrayal of traditional religious values.

Globalization. Process of becoming worldwide in scope.

Hadith. Traditions of the Prophet.

Hajj. Religious pilgrimage to Mecca.

Imperialism. Extending a nation's authority by territorial acquisition or by establishing economic and political hegemony over other nations.

Infidel. An unbeliever with respect to some religion.

Insurgency. Insurrection against an existing government, usually one's own.

Intifada. Uprising; esp. Palestinian against Israeli "occupation."

Irrendentist Islamic extremist. Subset of Islamic extremism; seeks to regain land ruled by non-Muslims or under occupation.

Islamic extremism. Individuals committed to restructuring political society in accordance with their vision of Islamic law and willing to use violence to achieve their goals; three types: irredentist; nationalist; transnational.

Islamism. Islamic activism; three types: political; missionary; extremist.

Islamist. Islamic activist.

Jihad. Struggle; two types: individual internal struggle against evil and temptation; holy war waged by Muslims against infidels.

Jihadist. Muslim involved in a jihad; note: Islamic extremists often identify themselves as jihadists.

Jahiliyyah. Ignorance; un-Islamic behavior.

Kafir. Unbelievers or infidels.

Kufr. Impious; unbelief.

Land of the Two Holy Places. Saudi Arabia.

Madrassa. Islamic religious school.

Moderate. Opposed to radical or extreme views; esp. in politics and religion.

Modernity. Characteristic of recent times or the present.

Mujahedeen. One who participates in jihad.

Nationalism. Devoted to the interests of a particular nation.

Nationalist Islamic extremist. Subset of Islamic extremism; focus is combating Muslim governments considered impious or apostate.

Salafism. Strict adherence to traditional Islamic values, religious orthodoxy, correct ritualistic practice, and moral issues.

Sharia. Islamic law.

Source. Thing or place from which something comes or arises; also origin, root cause.

Sunnah. Deeds or words of the Prophet.

Takfir. Excommunicate; declare as unbelievers.

Terrorism. Premeditated, politically motivated violence perpetrated against noncombatants by subnational groups or clandestine agents.

Transnational Islamic extremist. Subset of Islamic extremism; focus transcends national boundaries (e.g., combating the West); also called global terrorists or global jihadists.

Ulema. Religious scholars or clergy.

Umma. Community of Islamic believers.

Usury. Charging of interest for loaned money.

Wahhabism. Puritanical religious doctrine founded by 18th century evangelist Muhammed Abd al-Wahhab in Saudi Arabia.

Westernization. To convert to the customs of Western civilization.

# REFERENCES CITED

Bin Laden, Usama. circa 1995. *Message Regarding the Invasion of Arabia.* Quoted in Bruce Lawrence. *Messages to the World: The Statements of Osama bin Laden*, 15-16. London: Verso, 2005.

_____. 1996. *Declaration of War against the Americans Occupying the Land of the Two Holy Places.* Available from http://www.pbs.org/newshour/terrorism/international/fatwa_1996.html. Internet. Accessed 19 September 2006.

_____. 1998a. *World Islamic Front Declaration of Jihad against the Jews and the Crusaders.* Available from http://www.pbs.org/newshour/terrorism/international/fatwa_1998.html. Internet. Accessed 19 September 2006.

_____. 1998b. Interview with ABC News. Quoted in Public Broadcasting Service, 2002. *Frontline: Hunting Bin Laden.* Interview With Osama Bin Laden. Available from http://www.pbs.org/wgbh/pages/frontline/shows/Binladen/who/interview.html. Internet. Accessed 2 November 2006.

_____. 2001. *Letter to Al Jazeera's Kabul Bureau.* Quoted in Bruce Lawrence. *Messages to the World: The Statements of Osama bin Laden*, 135-136. London: Verso, 2005.

_____. 2002. *To the Americans.* Available from http://www.observer.guardian.co.uk/print/0,,4552895-110490,00.html. Internet. Accessed 18 December 2006.

_____. 2004. *Depose the Tyrants*, Message Posted to Global Islamic Front Website, 16 December. Quoted in Bruce Lawrence. *Messages to the World: The Statements of Osama bin Laden*, 245-248. London: Verso, 2005.

Bush, George W. 2005. *Veteran's Day Address.* Tobyhanna, Pennsylvania. 11 November. Available from http://www.whitehouse.gov/news/releases/2005/11/print/20051111-1.html. Internet. Accessed 2 November 2006.

_____. 2006. *Speech to Reserve Officers Association.* Washington, DC, 29 September. Available from http://www.roa.org/site/DocServer/1106_officer.pdf?docID=321. Internet. Accessed 23 November 2006.

Center for Strategic and International Studies. 2004. *Initial Findings.* The Transatlantic Dialogue on Terrorism, August. Available from http://www.csis.org/media/csis/pubs/0408_transatlantic.pdf. Internet. Accessed 14 December 2006.

Central Intelligence Agency. 2006. World Fact Book, Middle East Map. Available from https://www.cia.gov/cia/publications/factbook/reference_maps/pdf/middle_east.pdf. Internet. Accessed 15 December 2006.

Esposito, John L. 2003. *Unholy War: Terror in the Name of Islam.* New York: Oxford University Press.

Frechtling, Joy and Laure Sharp. 1997. *User-Friendly Handbook for Mixed Method Evaluations.* National Science Foundation. Available from http://www.nsf.gov/ pubs/1997/nsf97153/start.htm. Internet. Accessed 8 December 2006.

Habeck, Mary. 2006. *Knowing the Enemy: Jihadist Ideology and the War on Terror.* New Haven and London: Yale University Press.

Henzel, Christopher. 2005. *The Origins of al Qaeda's Ideology: Implications for US Strategy.* Available from http://www.army.mil/professionalwriting/volumes/ Volume3/October_2005/10_05_3_pf.html. Internet. Accessed 7 December 2006.

Illinois Institute of Technology. 2006. Government Publications Access. Ottoman Empire and Islamic Caliphate Maps. Available from http://www.gl.iit.edu/govdocs/ maps/maps.htm. Internet. Accessed 10 December 2006.

International Crisis Group. 2005. *Understanding Islamism,* Middle East/North African Report no. 37. Cairo; Brussels: International Crisis Group, 2005. Available from http://www.crisisgroup.org/home/index.cfm?id=3300&l=1. Internet. Accessed 25 September 2005.

Lawrence, Bruce ed. 2005. *Messages to the World: The Statements of Osama Bin Laden,*.Translated by James Howarth. London and New York: Verso Books.

Lewis, Bernard. 2004. *The Crisis of Islam: Holy War and Unholy Terror.* New York: Random House Publishing Group.

Mansfield, Laura. 2006. *His Own Words: A Translation of the Writings of Dr. Ayman Al Zawahiri.* TLG Publications.

National Intelligence Estimate. 2006. Declassified Key Judgments of the National Intelligence Estimate, *Trends in Global Terrorism: Implications for the United States,* dated April 2006. Available from http://www.dni.gov/press_releases/ Declassified_NIE_Key_Judgments.pdf. Internet. Accessed 1 December 2006.

Qutb, Sayyid. 1964. *Milestones* (or "Signposts") Damascus, Syria: Dar al-llm. (Originally Published in 1964; Numerous Editions Available).

RAND Corporation. 2004. *The Muslim World After 9/11*. Santa Monica, CA. Available from http://www.rand.org/pubs/monographs/MG246/. Internet. Accessed 1 November 2006.

Schoomaker, Peter J. 2006. Soldiers Must Have Needs Met. *Philadelphia Inquirer.* 21 November. Excerpts from the LeMoyne Leadership Lecture given 10 November at the Union League of Philadelphia.

The 9/11 Commission Report. 2004. *National Commission on Terrorist Attacks Upon the United States.* Available from http:www.9-11commission.gov. Internet. Accessed 21 September 2006.

United Nations. 2006a. *General Assembly Resolution 60/288.* The United Nations Global Counter-Terrorism Strategy. 20 September. Available from http://www.un.org/terrorism/strategy-counter-terrorism.html. Internet. Accessed 10 December 2006.

_____. 2006b. Counter-Terrorism Committee Executive Directorate Fact Sheet. Available from http://www.un.org/sc/ctc. Internet. Accessed 1 December 2006.

_____. 2006c. *Report of the High-level Group.* United Nations Alliance of Civilizations, Istanbul, Turkey, 13 November 2006. Available from http:/www. unaoc.org/repository/report.htm. Internet. Accessed 14 November 2006.

US Department of Defense. 2006a. *National Military Strategic Plan for the War on Terrorism.* Washington, D.C. Chairman of the Joint Chiefs of Staff. 1 February.

_____. 2006b. *Quadrennial Defense Report Review.* Washington, DC: Secretary of Defense. 6 February.

US Department of State. 2005. *Country Reports on Terrorism 2005* (released April 2006). Available from http://www.state.gov. Internet. Accessed 15 September 2006.

White House. 2006a. *The National Security Strategy of the United States of America.* March. Available from http://www.whitehouse.gov/infocus/nationalsecurity/. Internet. Accessed 10 September 2006.

_____. 2006b. *National Strategy for Combating Terrorism.* September. Available from http://www.whitehouse.gov/infocus/nationalsecurity/. Internet. Accessed 15 September 2006.

# REFERENCES CONSULTED

Congressional Research Service Report for Congress. 2005. *Al Qaeda Statements and Evolving Ideology,* RL33038. Washington, D.C.: Congressional Research Service, Library of Congress. Available from http://fpc.state.gov/fpc/48928.htm. Internet. Accessed 20 November 2006.

Congressional Research Service Report for Congress. 2005. *Al Qaeda Profile and Threat Assessment.* Washington, D.C.: Congressional Research Service, Library of Congress. Available from: http://fpc.state.gov/documents/organization/56106.pdf. Internet. Accessed 1 December 2006.

DeYoung, Karen. 2006. Letter Gives Glimpse of Al-Qaeda's Leadership. *Washington Post*, 2 October, 1.

Esposito, John L. 2006. It's the Policy Stupid. *Harvard International Review.* Available from http://hir.harvard.edu/articles/print.php?article=1453. Internet. Accessed 3 November 2006.

Gall, Carlotta. 2006. Pakistan's Support for Militants Threatens Region, Karzai Says. *New York Times*, 13 December, 20.

Gall, Carlotta and Ismail Khan. 2006. Taliban and Allies Tighten Grip in North of Pakistan. *New York Times*, 11 December, 1.

Gerges, Fawaz A. 2005. *The Far Enemy: Why Jihad Went Global.* New York: Cambridge University Press.

Hayden, Michael V. 2006. The Current Situation in Iraq and Afghanistan, General Michael V. Hayden, Central Intelligence Agency, Statement for the Record before the Senate Armed Services Committee, 15 November. Available from https://www.cia.gov/cia/public_affairs/speeches/2006/DCIA_SASC_testimony.html. Internet. Accessed 21 November 2006.

Harvey, Andrew, Ian Sullivan, and Ralph Groves. 2005. A Clash of Systems: An Analytical Framework to Demystify the Radical Islamist Threat. *Parameters.* Available from http://www.carlisle.army.mil/usawc/Parameters/05autumn/harvey.htm. Internet. Accessed 15 November 2006.

Hoffman, Bruce, and Rand Corporation. 2003. *Al Qaeda, Trends in Terrorism, and Future Possibilities: An Assessment.* Santa Monica, CA: RAND. Available from http://www.rand.org/pubs/papers/P8078/P8078.pdf. Internet. Accessed 1 November 2006.

Hughes, Karen. 2006. Where's the Outrage. *USA Today*, 12 September, 15.

Hutchings, Robert L. 2004. *The Sources of Terrorist Conduct.* Speech at the University of Virginia. 19 March. Available from http://www.dni.gov/nic/speeches_terrorist _conduct.html. Internet. Accessed 30 September 2006.

International Crisis Group. 2006. *Pakistan's Tribal Areas: Appeasing the Militants*, Asia Report no. 125. Islamabad; Brussels: International Crisis Group, 2006. Available from http://www.crisisgroup.org/home/index.cfm?id=4568&l=1. Internet. Accessed 23 December 2006.

Jaffe, Greg. 2006. A General's New Plan to Battle Radical Islam. *Wall Street Journal,* 2 September, 1.

Jordan, Mary. 2006. Britain's MI5 Warns of Rising Terror Threat. *Washington Post*, 11 November, 15.

Lewis, Bernard. 1998. License to Kill: Usama bin Ladin's Declaration of Jihad. *Foreign Affairs*, November/December 1998. Available from http://www.foreign affairs.org/19981101facomment1428/bernard-lewis/license-to-kill-usama-bin-ladin-s-declaration-of-jihad.html. Internet. Accessed 3 November 2006.

_____. 2002. *What Went Wrong? The Clash between Islam and Modernity in the Middle East.* New York: Oxford University Press.

_____. 2006. Islam and the West: A Conversation with Bernard Lewis. The Pew Forum on Religion and Public Life, Washington, DC, 27 April 2006. Available from http://pewforum.org/events/print.php?EventID=107. Internet. Accessed 3 November 2006.

Linzer, Dafna and Walter Pincus. 2006. Taliban, Al-Qaeda Resurge in Afghanistan. *Washington Post*, 16 November, 22.

McManus, Doyle. 2006. Is the U.S. Winning This War? *Los Angeles Times*, 10 September, 1.

Mogahed, Dalia. 2006. The Battle for Hearts and Minds: Moderate vs. Extremist Views in the Muslim World. A Gallup Poll Special Report. The Gallup Organization, Princeton, NJ.

Musharraf, Pervez. 2004. A Plea for Enlightened Moderation. *Washington Post,* 1 June, A23. Available from: http://www.washingtonpost.com/ac2/wp-dyn/A5081-2004May31?language=printer. Internet. Accessed 7 December 2006.

National Intelligence Council. 2004. Mapping the Global Future, Report of the National Intelligence Council's 2020 Project. Available from http://www.dni.gov/nic/NIC_Globaltrend2020.html. Internet. Accessed 30 September 2006.

Negroponte, John D. 2006. *Annual Threat Assessment of the Director of National Intelligence for the Senate Armed Services Committee.* (Statement made 28 February 2006). Available online at http://www.dni.gov/testimonies/printer_friendly/20060228_testimony_print.htm. Internet. Accessed 8 September 2006.

Priest, Dana and Ann Scott Tyson. 2006. Bin Laden Trail 'Stone Cold.' *Washington Post*, 10 September, 1.

Rohde, David. 2006. Al Qaeda Finds Its Center of Gravity. *New York Times*, 10 September, WK3.

Rumsfeld, Donald H. 2006a. FY 2007 Posture Statement Before The Senate Armed Services Committee, Washington, DC, 7 February 2006. Available from http://www.defenselink.mil/Speeches/Speech.aspx?SpeechID=29. Internet. Accessed 9 August 2006.

_____. 2006b. Speech to US Army War College, Carlisle Barracks, Pennsylvania, 27 March 2006. Available from http://www.defenselink.mil/Speeches/Speech.Aspx?SpeechID=22. Internet. Accessed 9 August 2006.

_____. 2006c. Address at the 88th Annual American Legion National Convention, Salt Lake City, Utah, 29 August 2006. Available from http://www.defenselink.mil/Speeches/Speech.aspx?SpeechID=1033. Internet. Accessed 31 August 2006.

_____. 2006d. A Force for Good. *Wall Street Journal*, 11 September, 14.

Sennott, Charles M. 2006. Radical Teachings in Pakistan Schools. *Boston Globe*, 29 September, 1.

Sniffin, Peter R. 2002. The Impact of a Theology upon a Political Ideology and Resulting Threats to United States Strategic Interests. Master of Military Art and Science Thesis, US Army Command and General Staff College.

Turabian, Kate L. 1996. *A Manual for Writers.* 6th ed. Chicago: University of Chicago Press.

US Army. Command and General Staff College. 2004. ST 20-10, *Master of Military Art and Science (MMAS) Research and Thesis.* Ft. Leavenworth, KS: USA CGSC, July.

US Government Accounting Office. 2005. Information on Agencies' Efforts to Address Islamic Extremism. Washington, D.C. Available from http://www.gao.gov/cgi-bin/getrpt?GAO-05-852. Internet. Accessed 1 November 2006.

Walk, Kerry. 1998. *How to Write a Comparative Analysis*. Writing Center at Harvard University. Available from http://www.fas.harvard.edu/~wricntr/documents/ CompAnalysis.html. Internet. Accessed 5 December 2006.

Whitlock, Craig. 2006. US Faces Obstacles to Freeing Detainees. *Washington Post*, 17 October, 1.

Wike, Richard, and Nilanthi Samaranayake. 2006. Where Terrorism Finds Support in the Muslim World. Pew Research Center, Washington, DC, 23 May. Available from http://www.pewresearch.org/obdeck/?ObDeckID=26. Internet. Accessed 3 November 2006.

Wright, Lawrence. 2002. The Man behind Bin Laden: How an Egyptian Doctor Became a Master of Terror. *The New Yorker*, 16 September. Available from http://www. Newyorker.com/printables/fact/620916fa_fact2. Internet. Accessed 18 December 2006.

Zawahiri, Ayman. 2005. Letter from Zawahiri to Al Zarqawi. (July 2005). Available at the Director of National Intelligence website. Available from http://www.dni.gov/ letter_in_english.pdf. Internet. Accessed 15 September 2006.

www.ingramcontent.com/pod-product-compliance
Lightning Source LLC
Chambersburg PA
CBHW081328310526
45789CB00018B/2516